History of England

Leon Amiel Publisher
New York

Concise History of Great Nations
General Editor: Otto Zierer

David Mountfield England

Contents

Dust jacket: The battle of Hastings.
A Flemish miniature of the 15th century.
Title page: London's river, the Thames, with
St. Paul's Cathedral in the background.

Credits:
Bibliothèque Nationale de Paris: 2, 3, 10, 19, 22a, b, 23a, b, 25a, 34, 36, 37, 48a, 54, 55, 58, 59, 63, 64, 68, 69, 70, 71, 72, 76, 77, 78, 82a, b, 83, 84, 92, 93a, b, 94, 96, 97, 99, 107, British Authority: 9, 11, 13, 17, 26, 27, 28a, b, 31, 33, 34, 35, 37, 38, 55, Boyer/Viollet: 91, Giraudon: 15, 21, 24, 38, 39, 40, 46, 51, 59, 77, 79, 87, 98, 99a, b, 100, Keystone: 114, 116a, b, 118, 119a, b, 120, 121, 122, Lauros/Giraudon: 53, 66, 89a, b, Musées Nationaux de France: 44, 48b, 49, 50, 51, 52a, 53, 56, 57, 61, 65, 67, 73, 76, 81, 94, 95, 101, Roger-Viollet: 14, 18, 52b, 63a, b, 65, 74, 75, 85, 90, 102a, b, 103, 107, 109, 110a, b, 111, 112a, b, 115, Snark International: jacket, 25b, 38, 40, 42, 43, 45, 60, 68, 72, 104, 108, 109, 116, 117, Unedi: 9, 12, 13, 21, 24, 29, 32, 41, 47, 48, 49, 50, 53, 86, 88, 105.

Published 1978 by Leon Amiel Publisher
31 West 46th Street,
New York, N.Y. 10036,
U.S.A.

Library of Congress Catalog Card No. 77-73095
I.S.B.N. No. 0-8148-0674-0

© Media Books S. A., Nyon, 1978
Printed in West-Germany by Mohndruck Reinhard Mohn OHG, Gütersloh

1 Introduction

The British Isles consist of two large islands, plus a number of small ones, lying off the north-west coast of Europe. The larger of the two islands, Great Britain (England, Scotland and Wales), covers an area of almost 230,000 square kilometres. Together with the province of Northern Ireland (14,000 square kilometres) it constitutes the United Kingdom.

Situated on the edge of the world's greatest land mass and divided from it by a narrow but significant stretch of the sea, Britain has always maintained a certain separateness from European civilization, of which it is part. In ancient times it was briefly included in the Roman world, but remained comparatively unaffected by the Roman occupation. The Norman Conquest and the bonds of the Church tied it more closely to medieval Christendom, and in the 12th and 13th centuries England was a more intimate part of Europe than it has been at any other time until the present. Two developments in the 16th century divorced England from Europe: the Reformation which severed the connection with the Roman Church, and the development of trans-Atlantic sea routes.

The expansion of Europe in the Americas and other parts of the world brought England from the distant fringe of Western civilization to a position near the centre, well-placed to take advantage of opportunities in the New World. Henceforward, England looked not towards Europe, but outward towards more distant lands across the sea. Growing steadily more prosperous, the English avoided European entanglements and hazarded their future on shipping, trade and colonies. Such was their success that they came to dominate world commerce in the 18th century and created a material environment in which the industrial revolution could flourish a generation earlier than in any other country, making Great Britain the most prosperous and most powerful country in the world in the 19th century.

It is unlikely that the English could have achieved their material success if they had not also led the way in evolving a form of government in which an efficient executive was combined with popular sovereignty. The English bourgeois revolution took place a century before the French Revolution, and so Britain avoided the period of despotic monarchy that most of its neighbours experienced in the 18th century. The new society that took root in America in the 17th century developed a remarkably democratic character—more democratic, in fact, than the mother country.

Of all that the English have bequeathed to the world (and it is arguable that the aims and institutions of the world today owe more to the English than to any other people), it is perhaps this tradition of liberal parliamentary government that is most important.

2 Birth of the English Nation -979

In 55 BC Julius Caesar decided to invade Britain. He was provoked partly by the aid given by the British to their relations in northern Gaul, and at the same time he hoped to record a triumph which would strengthen his standing at Rome. Perhaps he was also attracted by booty—the slaves, gold and pearls that Britain might provide. But his invasion nearly ended in disaster, and although, in the following year, he succeeded in pushing north of the Thames with the help of some British tribes, he effected no conquest and rapidly withdrew. In Rome, Cicero made scathing remarks about the paucity of the treasure that resulted from Caesar's foray, while in Gaul, Vercingetorix seized the moment to launch a revolt against Roman rule. For one hundred years afterwards, Rome left the British alone.

The disparaging eye of the Roman invader saw the British as a race of primitives, barbarians who painted their bodies blue with woad. But in this case Caesar exaggerated. The British were not savages, nor were they entirely unfamiliar with Latin culture. The Belgae, a Celtic people who settled in Britain only one or two generations before Caesar's invasion, were closely in touch with developments in northern Gaul and themselves touched by Roman customs, while trade contacts between Britain and the Mediterranean world dated from a much earlier time.

The Celts were not the original inhabitants of Britain, although people now living in the so-called "Celtic fringe" (Scotland, Wales and southwest England) sometimes talk as if they were. Like the Romans themselves, the Celts were merely one of a succession of invaders who moved into Britain from the east. The great stone buildings of Stonehenge, built about 1800–1500 BC had been standing a thousand years when the first Celts arrived. But when Pytheas, the first commentator on British affairs, visited the island about 320 BC in search of the origins of the tin trade, he described the inhabitants simply as Celts, and incidentally remarked that they were "unusually hospitable . . . and gentle in their manner", a description that would have surprised many later visitors.

The arrival of the Belgae hastened the development of Celtic society, especially in the military sphere: their hill forts were substantial by continental standards, although the chariot warfare practised by the Belgae was already out of date, as the Roman legions were to prove. The area under agriculture expanded with the help of better tools, and a coinage based on gold was introduced. These signs of growing prosperity undoubtedly attracted Roman attention, though Caesar and his officers would not have been impressed by what is for us the most exciting aspect of ancient British culture – Celtic art, with its bold, abstract designs, especially in bronze and enamel work. Caesar made no comment on Celtic art (perhaps he did not see any) and he was predictably scornful of Celtic religion, dominated by a powerful priestly caste, the Druids, who controlled justice and education, such as they were.

During the hundred years between Caesar's sorties and the Roman invasion of AD 43, the population, swollen by refugees from northern Gaul, grew swiftly and, as warring tribes gradually coalesced, signs of political contralization were unmistakeable. The coins of Cunobelin (better known as Shakespeare's Cymbeline), who ruled the Catuvellauni in the south-east in the early 1st century, proclaimed him *Rex Britonnum* (king of the Britons).

Lowland Britain benefitted economically from proximity to the great Roman empire without concomitant political domination. Roman influence was considerable and British rulers—certainly Cunobelin—were well-disposed towards Rome. The geographer Strabo remarked that the island was "almost" a Roman colony even before the invasion of the Emperor Claudius in AD 43.

Like other invaders both earlier and

later, the Romans conquered Lowland Britain (roughly equivalent to modern England) without great difficulty, but stumbled when they reached the mountainous regions of the west and north.

Many people in Lowland Britain, already part-Romanized, welcomed the imperial take-over, and it was the Romans' own intolerance that provoked the revolt of the British queen Boudicca (Boadicea) in their rear while they were advancing into Wales in AD 61. Boudicca, with her long golden hair and knife-wheeled cha-

riots, was soon killed and the revolt suppressed. Thereafter, the *pax Romana* descended upon Lowland Britain, but the mountainous uplands were another matter. The Romans took over thirty years to subdue Wales; they wisely ignored Ireland, and they never penetrated far into the south-west peninsula of England (Devon and Cornwall). The Romans had their own supplies of tin and the Cornish tin mines held no attraction.

The greatest trouble came from the north. Scotland, rugged and remote, successfully resisted the legions. After the plans of the able Agricola had been cancelled on the grounds of expense, the Romans never managed to pacify the fierce Picts of Caledonia (Scotland). The Emperor Hadrian, bowing to the inevitable, ordered construction of the wall named after him—a great stone barrier three metres wide and five metres high with regularly spaced forts and towers—between the Tyne and the Solway. Begun in 122, it was the largest single construction job of the Roman Empire. Hadrian's successor, Antoninus, built another wall, of earth, farther north between Clyde and Forth, but it did not hold for long, and in spite of occasional Roman sor-

Hadrian's Wall marked the approximate northern limit of the Roman Empire. It was about 115 km long and, as additional protection, had a ditch about three metres deep on its northern side.

The remains of one of the forts built at frequent intervals along Hadrian's Wall. Defence of the frontier was expensive, and the Romans might have done better to follow up Agricola's plan of conquest.

Right: Remains of the Roman baths at Aquae Sulis, better known as Bath.
Below: An Army approaching the gates of London; from a medieval manuscript.

ties northward, the boundary of the empire remained where Hadrian had fixed it.

Thus the Roman occupation covered an area equivalent to modern England and Wales except for a narrow strip in the north and the extreme south-west. But only about half that area—the more prosperous, south-eastern half—belonged to Roman civilization. In the north and west the Roman presence was that of an occupying army, in constant danger of outbreaks by people like the Brigantes of Yorkshire or the fierce tribes of the Welsh hills. From their bridgehead on the Thames at Londinium (London) the Romans' roads radiated confidently outwards, but as they reached farther into the west and north their military purpose became ever more plain and the tramp of the legions' feet echoed through the land with diminishing assurance.

In spite of the grain and wool that it exported, Britain was an expensive colony. The least of the imperial provinces, it required about one-tenth of the army to protect it, and it is not surprising that it was regarded without much enthusiasm in Rome.

In some respects, the colonial connection suited neither party. There were no real towns in Britain before the Romans came, but Roman society was essentially urban, depending on the organization and capacity of a large empire for the sustenance of its splendid cities. Such a society was hard to adapt to a country covered by more forests than fields. In this and in other ways, Roman civilization was thoroughly alien to Britain. Conditions in the Mediterranean world were very different from conditions in northern Europe, and the Romans found they had to adapt the form of their villas to suit a colder, damper climate. The

up with the kind of political authority exercised by the Druids. The Druids were destroyed; but Celtic gods lingered on alongside Roman gods, sometimes merging with them. The Celtic goddess Sulis, whose "waters" at Bath were a popular Roman resort, became associated with the Minerva of the Romans; Mars, the Roman god of war, became incongruously the god of healing.

Nor did the official acceptance of Christianity banish the pagan gods; there are few known examples of Christian churches in Roman Britain, but plenty of evidence of the continuing existence of pagan worship in the Christian era.

Strangely, the Christian religion, adopted so late by the empire, was one of Rome's few legacies to Britain (the roads, which eased the paths of later invaders, were another). Though it was to disappear from Lowland Britain, Celtic Christianity continued unbroken in remoter parts of the British Isles from Roman times to the coming of St Augustine (597), and in spite of the lack of zeal shown by the British in embracing Christianity in the 4th century, the greatest man of late Roman Britain was a bull-necked monk, Pelagius, whose humane rejection of the doctrine of Original Sin shook the Christian Church to its foundations.

As Alaric and his Visigoths approached the Eternal City, the legions in Britain were withdrawn in 410 to protect the motherland. The Emperor Honorius wrote to the Romano-British leaders informing them that for the time being they would have to look after their own defence.

The Roman retreat, which Honorius and no doubt the British themselves regarded as temporary, did not mean an immediate collapse of Romano-British society, but it did leave

British themselves may have been willing or eager to become good Romans—and in the cities even the workmen and slaves seem to have spoken a kind of basic Latin—but the process of Romanization was, considering the long time span of Roman occupation, quite superficial.

The reason was partly a simple matter of numbers. The Romano-British ruling class was very small: the sites of only about 600 villas are known, and although others may be discovered and some may have vanished altogether, the total number must have been far less than one thousand. As for the towns, the total population of all but three (London, St Alban's and Colchester) was less than 5,000 and it is clear from excavations

at Roman Silchester that the town there never expanded to the size anticipated by its planners. Even in heavily populated areas like northern Kent, large tracts of adjacent land bear no trace of Roman settlement.

The Romano-British ruling class was small but it was prosperous. Before the legions were withdrawn, they enjoyed a standard of living that was not to be equalled in England until the 16th century or later. They possessed other advantages—administrative unity, safety from attack—that were to disappear for a long, long time after the Romans departed.

In matters of religion, the Romans were comparatively tolerant, though they drew the line at human sacrifice and were certainly not prepared to put

There was an affinity between Celtic and Anglo-Saxon art, for example in their liking for abstract design and fine metalwork, like this chased and gilded bronze.

the British in a very difficult situation. Saxon raids, which had begun in the 3rd century, were increasing. The British had no army, and their defences were organized to repel attack from the north, not from the south-east. It ist not surprising that Romano-British society was overwhelmed; the surprise is that it lasted so long—long after all contact with Rome was broken in about 450.

By that time the Saxon raids had become a migration, and the Romano-British leaders were compelled to retreat westward to the safety of the mountains where, augmented by Irish immigrants, Celtic culture enjoyed a revival. But the retreating British put up something more than a desperate rearguard action. After the death of Ambrosius, "the last Roman", early in the 6th century, they fought back successfully for a time. Their leader in this shadowy period (there are no contemporary writings) was the prototype of the legendary King Arthur, whose small forces of well-disciplined, armoured soldiers inflicted some defeats on the advancing Saxons.

The chief cause of the collapse of British resistance after Arthur's death (about 540) seems to have been not the Anglo-Saxon invasion but internecine quarrels arising from the ecclesiastical division between the Pelagians and the adherents of orthodox "Roman" Christianity. Within a short time, Romano-British culture virtually disappeared; the Anglo-Saxons advanced up the valleys, clearing the trees with their hefty German axes, and gradually settled down to become, in a few generations, recognisably "English".

The name "Anglo-Saxons" is still sometimes used as a synonym—in the mouth of the late President de Gaulle not a very friendly one—for the white,

English-speaking peoples. Certainly the Anglo-Saxons have formed the largest element in the English (but not Welsh or Scottish) nation, but the English—and indeed the Scots—are even more of a mixture than most European peoples, while the original Anglo-Saxons themselves were a conglomerate race. They were closer to the Celts than some modern "Celts" would like to think; their art, which shows little trace of Classical conventions, has obvious affinities with Celtic art.

The Anglo-Saxon settlement marks no sharp break in the history of Britain. Town life was already decaying in the Romano-British period: the splendid baths at Aquae Sulis (Bath) were probably already a ruin when the

Saxons arrived. The institution of kingship was known in Britain as well as north Germany. The open-field system, in which large fields were cultivated in strips, was probably already present, although the Anglo-Saxons, with better axes, stronger needs and larger numbers, made great advances in land-clearing: place names in most of England today testify to the permanence of their settlements. Not only the names of places but the Anglo-Saxon language itself survived, to form the basis of modern English (though Anglo-Saxon is incomprehensible except to students of it).

One major innovation of the Anglo-Saxons to Roman Britain was their military organization. Gone were the palmy days of a professional army.

15

The early Anglo-Saxon settlers carried sword, shield and spear, and were expected to use them on behalf of their lord.

The local Anglo-Saxon lords were at first little more than tribal chiefs. Their authority was based partly on kinship, but more on their reputation as leaders in war, for in their disordered society martial prowess was the most necessary virtue. A man's loyalty to his lord, emphasised by Alfred's laws in the 9th century, was the principle on which Anglo-Saxon society was founded, and prefigured feudal relationships.

But the Anglo-Saxons were not a race of freebooters commanded by warlords, and although the early Anglo-Saxon *coerl* had more personal freedom than the serf of feudal times, theirs was an autocratic society, with a king and a class of nobles. In time, those who laboured became dependent on those who fought, and the status of the ordinary peasant farmer was imperceptibly debased. The rights over land granted by the king as his only means of reward to his followers assisted this process, and as taxation became heavier, the peasant farmer offered his labour instead of the rent due in kind to the lord who gave him security.

There is a certain grimness in Anglo-Saxon society. As they gathered in their log-built halls and huts, telling their tales of resolute Nordic heroes, contemplating their fearsome gods (whose names are commemorated in the days of the week), and foreseeing the chaos against which even the gods offered only temporary protection, one imagines more determination than cheerfulness, more gloom than glee.

Such attitudes were not unreasonable. The metaphysical chaos imagined by the Anglo-Saxons mirrored the actual chaos of their times, when war, public and private, was incessant, and life was dominated by the unrelenting struggle with nature. But the hardness and poverty of life in Anglo-Saxon England must not be exaggerated. The discovery in the 1930s of the treasures of the Sutton Hoo burial ship in East Anglia, revealed riches hitherto unsuspected in that early kingdom, and confirmed the existence of a prosperous trade with the continent.

When Pope Gregory's emissary, St Augustine, arrived in Kent in 597 to restore the link broken a century and a half earlier, he was welcomed by people eager to embrace the Christian religion. A Northumbrian convert, somewhat later, accounted for his own conversion by an attractive simile, Comparing the liefe of a man to the flight of a sparrow through the warmed and lighted hall of the king, while outside a winter storm rages: "The sparrow, flying in at one door and immediately out of another, while he is within, is safe from the wintry tempest; but after a short space of fair weather, he immediately vanishes out of your sight, passing from winter into winter again. So this life of man appears for a little while, but of what is to follow, or what went before, we know nothing at all. If, therefore, this new doctrine tells us something more certain, it seems justly to deserve to be followed".

Although Christianity had disappeared from Anglo-Saxon England, it had not vanished from the British Isles. Northern England was reconverted not by Roman missionaries, but by Celtic Christians from the monastery on Iona (an island off south-west Scotland), who established another "Holy Isle" on Lind-isfarne, off the Northumbrian coast. Pope Gregory had advised Augustine, on founding the English Church at Canterbury, to "make a careful selection of anything that you have found either in the Roman, or the Gallic, or any other Church which may be more acceptable to God" and, after some sharp exchanges, agreement between the Celtic and Roman Churches was reached at the Synod of Whitby in 663. Although it was a reasonably friendly agreement, its ultimate result was the victory of Rome over the less disciplined, less worldly, Celtic Church.

Thereafter, the English Church prospered extraordinarily. In the 8th century it was the most vigorous Church in northern Europe: much of Germany was converted by English missionaries, and the scholar-poet Alcuin of York became Charlemagne's principal assistant in educating the Franks.

The reconversion of England to Christianity during the 7th century marks the reappearance of written historical records (and, less happily, the disappearance of pagan burials that provide archaeologists with such interesting data). Latin culture soon found splendid expression in the "Northumbrian renaissance", of which the outstanding figure was Bede. Although he left his monastery at Jarrow only twice during his life (673–735), Bede displayed in his *Ecclesiastical History of the English Nation* a degree of learning and common sense, plus humour and tolerance, that makes him a loved and honoured forefather of English historiography.

During the 8th century, the predominance of Northumbria among the Anglo-Saxon kingdoms (almost the only time in history when the centre of power lay in the north) declined: it was replaced by the midland kingdom of

Saints pictured on the coffin of St Cuthbert, 698, in Durham Cathedral.
The coffin also contained a superbly worked stole which has survived
thirteen centuries, an early masterpiece of English needlework.

Vile deeds at the early court of Wessex: the King's mistress poisoned by the Queen.

Mercia. The greatest of the kings of Mercia, Offa, who reigned 757–796, corresponded on terms of equality with Charlemagne, although the Frankish emperor showed some doubts about a marriage alliance. Offa founded mints and issued the first nation-wide currency since Roman times; but he is chiefly remembered for building "Offa's Dyke", an earthen rampart, still visible, that marked the border of Mercia with Wales.

It was neither Northumbria nor Mercia but a third Anglo-Saxon kingdom, Wessex, which was to succeed in uniting England permanently as a centralized state.

At the time, nothing seemed less likely. Anglo-Saxon England appeared doomed to be overrun by a vast Danish army which invaded East Anglia in 865. The Danes had been raiding eastern England for many years, but never before had they come in such numbers. In 867 they destroyed Northumbrian resistance. Half Mercia fell to them, and in 871 they launched themselves in full strength against the kingdom of Wessex. In the same year, after the deaths of his father and three elder brothers, Alfred became king of Wessex.

Alfred, England's Charlemagne, is the only English king to whom posterity has given the title, "The Great". It is an honour beyond dispute. Perhaps if we knew more about 9th-century England, the figure of Alfred himself might not bulk so large, but there can be little doubt that if ever a kingdom were saved by one man, that kingdom was England and that man was Alfred.

Already at 21 a seasoned warrior when he became king, Alfred's first task—the first duty of every medieval king—was to defeat the enemy. In 871 the Danes were checked, and withdrew

to their base at Reading. In 876 the onslaught was renewed under Guthrum, an able strategist, and Alfred was forced to take refuge among the marshes of Somerset. It was at this time, according to a legend possibly invented by later panegyricists, that the king sought shelter in the hut of a peasant woman who, not recognising him, left him to watch her loaves baking.

Brooding on his plight, Alfred allowed the loaves to burn and on her return the enraged woman struck him.

Burned loaves or not, Alfred regrouped his men with surprising speed, outgeneralled the Danes and defeated them conclusively. Guthrum accepted Christian baptism and the frontier of Scandinavian territory (the "Danelaw") was agreed by both sides

A statue of Alfred the Great stands guard over Winchester, ancient capital of Wessex.

in 886. Alfred saw that to drive the Danes out of England was impossible and perhaps undesirable. He hoped to persuade them to settle down and become relatively peaceful farmers, believing that enemies become less menacing when their bellies are full.

Viking attacks were renewed from France in 892, but Alfred's defensive innovations, which included fortified towns and the building of the first English fleet, had vastly improved the position, and Wessex stood firm. By that time Alfred was recognised as king by all the English.

Alfred's greatness does not rest on his generalship alone. A highly intelligent, humane and pious man, he sought to raise the standard of civilization among his people by means of education, religion and just laws. Having visited Rome as a child, he was determined that the English should be given the benefits of Latin culture. All free-born English boys should at least learn to read English, and as there was nothing for them to read, Alfred set to work to translate standard works into Anglo-Saxon. Though he attracted many scholars to his court, he did much of the translating work himself. (In his later years he became less and less literal: he inserted the story of Othere's voyage to the Arctic, told to him presumably by the great Scandinavian traveller himself, into a work by the Spanish-born historian of the 5th century, Orosius, and he employed homely images of the plough and the axe to illustrate the erudite works of Latin scholars).

At his court in Winchester, Alfred drew up the first system of English laws. He explained his eclectic method of selection with typical simplicity: "I, King Alfred, collected these [laws] together and ordered those that I liked to be written down. I showed them to my councillors and they said they were all pleased to observe them''. He added, however, that some of his laws might not be useful indefinitely, and when the time was right, they should be changed. Alfred also founded the *Anglo-Saxon Chronicle*, a "current history" of England which gives an invaluable description of his own and later times, though it is naturally not very helpful for the earlier Anglo-Saxon period.

Alfred's was a mind of wide interests, more characteristic of the 16th than the 9th century, but practical and down-to-earth (among other achievements, he invented a kind of water clock). He left his own epitaph: "I desired to live worthily all my life, and leave to the men who should come after my memory in good works".

That this modest hope was so thoroughly fulfilled was partly the result of the abilities of his immediate descendants. His son Edward and his formidable daughter Ethelflaed ably contained the Danes, and his grandson Athelstan made himself king of virtually all England in fact as well as name. There was one *Witan* (an assembly of noble advisers, nominated by the king) for the whole country, and Athelstan was at times vaguely acknowledged as their overlord by Celtic rulers in Scotland and Wales. His many sisters were married to Charles the Simple, to the Emperor Otto I, and other continental kings.

But unfortunately for the kingdom of Old England, the high quality of the rulers of the House of Wessex was not maintained, and when the second great Danish invasion began, no Alfred emerged from the Somerset marshes to hold the Danes at bay.

Opposite above: Edmund, king of East Anglia, was murdered by Danish invaders in 870. He became the St Edmund of Bury St Edmunds. The House of Wessex was briefly restored in the person of Edward the Confessor, pictured right in the Bayeux Tapestry.

3 Norman England 979-1154

The Danish invasions at the end of the 10th century coincided with the reign of the weak and unpopular Ethelred (979–1016), who was forced to purchase a fragile security for his throne by enormous payments of "Danegeld". These bribes to the invaders only postponed the inevitable, and the apostate Danish king Sweyn soon resolved on the complete conquest of England. Sweyn died in 1014 before he could carry out his plan, but the standard was picked up by his son Cnut. As it turned out, no conquest was necessary, for the deaths of Ethelred and, a few months later, of his more capable son Edmund Ironside, left Cnut without a rival. England became a part of Cnut's large Scandinavian empire.

Against expectations, Cnut turned out to be a sensible and enlightened king. He soothed the English by adopting Christianity and marrying Ethelred's widow, and his good sense is reflected in the story (perhaps base-less) of how he sat on the beach until the tide came in to discountenance his obsequious courtiers, who had told him that at the command of so great a king the sea itself would retreat.

One feature of Cnut's reign boded ill for the future. So large was his empire that he was compelled to delegate authority to the increasingly powerful earls who ruled their own regions without much royal interference. England might well have split, like Germany, into a number of petty states had not this development been nipped in the bud by the Norman Conquest.

Cnut's two sons lacked their father's authority and on the death of the second in 1042 the House of Wessex was restored, without much trouble, in the person of Edward the Confessor (son of Ethelred). Although Edward was not the saintly, unworldly character that his surname (and many books) suggest, he was unable or unwilling to check the power of the greatest of the earls, Godwine, who was chiefly re-sponsible for securing his crown for him. But being half Norman by birth and having spent most of his life in Normandy, Edward balanced the

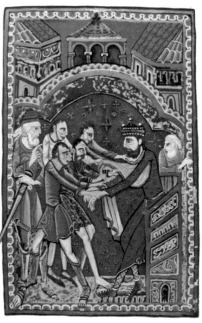

Below left: St Dunstan, one of the greatest figures of the early English Church, crowning King Edward, who was to be murdered in 978.
Below centre: Cnut demonstrating to his attendants that they were wrong to suggest the tide would recede in awe rather than encroach upon so mighty a king.

Below right: William prepares to invade. The pictures on these pages come from old French prints.

power of Godwine by bringing in Norman lieutenants. He appointed a Norman archbishop of Canterbury, and he bestowed the important military post of warden of the Welsh Marches on the Norman Earl Ralph. As a further blow against Godwine, Edward, who had married the earl's daughter, failed to provide an heir.

Nevertheless, before Edward died in January, 1066, he recognised Godwine's son Harold as his heir. Harold was as likely a candidate as anyone, but his claim was not strong and it was immediately and hotly questioned by William, duke of Normandy.

Though only the illegitimate son of Duke Robert of Normandy, William had a genealogical claim to the English throne that was as good as Harold's; but he based his right of succession on two alleged promises. In the first place, he said that Edward the Confessor had willed the Crown to him. Edward indeed had probably done so some 25 years before, but at the last Edward had recommended Harold. In any

Right: According to William the Conqueror, Harold had renounced his claim to the throne when visiting Normandy ten years before the Conquest, but Harold possibly was forced into his renunciation.

case, the crown was not in the king's will as it was, strictly speaking, elective: the assent of the *Witan* was required. In the second place, William said that Harold had acknowledged his claim two years earlier, when Harold had visited Normandy in rather shadowy circumstances. This also may have been true, but Harold's oath to

Right and below: The Bayeux Tapestry recorded in comic-strip form the conquest of England by William of Normandy in 72 scenes. The tapestry is a strip of linen about 75 m long, embroidered in coloured wools now browned by age.

William had without doubt been extracted under pressure.

The matter was decided, as such matters usually are, by force. With his host of Normans and Bretons, William landed in England while Harold was in the north defeating a Norwegian invasion. Harold hurried south and, near Hastings, unwisely offered battle to the Normans; he might have done better to starve them out. Still, his strong position on a hill should have proved impregnable if Norman feints had not succeeded in luring his infantry from their position. Harold was killed, struck in the head by an ar-

events in a way that almost nothing else—certainly not the Roman occupation—has done.

In the first place, England was drawn back into the European system. William did not, of course, forsake his continental possessions when he became king of England, and although he divided England and Normandy between two of his sons, the division was shortlived. The continental involvements of the English monarchy that sprang from the accession of a foreign dynasty form one of the major themes of medieval European history; England's last continental possession was not lost until the middle of the 16th century.

The Norman Conquest resulted in an almost total change in landholding in England. All land was held ultimately of the king, who distributed it among his Norman followers (carefully ensuring that the largest estates were widely scattered, so that no man possessed a substantial power-base). By 1086 William's tenants-in-chief were almost all Normans; less than two per cent of Anglo-Saxon landholders remained in possession. As a sign of the change, clean-cut stone castles rose threateningly at every strong-

row according to the graphic evidence of the Bayeux tapestry, and William's way lay open to London. The English magnates, disunited, submitted in a rather craven fashion, and William became king of England.

William's first priority was to establish his constitutional rectitude. There was to be no talk of a "Conquest". He had come, he assured the English lords, to restore the good laws of King Edward and to uphold the constitution. To begin with, he moved gently and interfered as little as possible with Anglo-Saxon institutions; but resentment against the Normans was not quelled by William's propaganda and a succession of revolts provoked William into harshly repressive action. In the north of the country his troops created devastation on a scale that England, by comparison with most European countries, has seldom suffered. Hardly a building was left standing between York and Durham.

The date of the Norman Conquest—1066—is the one date that every Englishman remembers. That is appropriate, for the Conquest was probably the most significant event in English history. It altered the course of

The old St Cross Hospital at Winchester. The ancient Anglo-Saxon capital receded in importance during Norman times.

point across the country; while in the fastest-growing towns, deliberately selected as the seats of bishops, great cathedrals began to rise, scarcely distinguishable, in the early stages of construction, from the castles nearby, and thus emphasising the Norman alliance between Church and State.

The extraordinary building programme of the Normans was one mark of their efficiency. No less remarkable was the compilation of what is known as Domesday Book (1086), a kind of inventory of the country, listing the landholders and subtenants, local rights and customs and various other matters—in some places even the number of livestock—as they were in Edward the Confessor's time and as they were twenty years later, at the time the survey was carried out. Among other things, Domesday Book is a treasure trove for historians of 11th-century England (though it is incomprehensible to non-specialists).

The enormous variety of social and economic circumstances revealed by Domesday Book should prevent anyone speaking of a "feudal system" in England. Feudalism is a concept that can lead to misunderstanding, especially in England, and the word is often used in the way that Humpty Dumpty used a word: it meant what he intended it should mean. The Normans did not suddenly introduce feudalism to England; nor did they impose one static form of social organisation on another equally static. The Middle Ages, like any other period, were a time of change, and change was both more rapid and more profound than contemporaries realised. Not only did customs vary between one county and the next, or between one manor and the next, they changed in the course of time. The payment of *scutage* (shield money) instead of military service was

Canterbury Cathedral was without an archbishop for four years under William II.

already relatively common within 100 years of the Conquest.

However, Anglo-Norman society had certain basic features. It was a society founded on personal dependence, with a small, military class at the top. Rights of property (the only measure of wealth and social status) were divided and subdivided like a descending pyramid, from the king downwards. The whole structure was maintained by a variety of institutions that regulated the relationship between lord and vassal (tenant), in which the vassal performed a service, usually military service, in exchange for his land. The basic unit was the manor, where freeman and serfs performed labour services and paid rent in kind, while tilling their own strips in the large open fields.

This type of society was not alien to England. The seeds of it at least existed in pre-Norman times, and though Norman customs were different, for instance in the essentially military character of feudal relationships, all the Normans had to do was to release potentials already present. Many Anglo-Saxon institutions, such as the territorial courts, were left unchanged. William, after all, represented himself as the preserver of Old English laws, which the "usurper" Harold had briefly endangered. He wanted to upset no apple cart—unless, of course, it was a serious obstruction.

Not everyone, even in the 11th century, worked on the land. There were fishermen and sailors and, under the Norman kings, town life grew rapidly. In the towns there was more freedom for the individual—at least as long as he belonged to the guild merchant, which excluded strangers and jealously guarded the charter and privileges of the town. Those privileges outlived the feudal rights of the magnates.

William I had undertaken the conquest of England with the blessing of the Pope, but once safely established, he kept the Pope at a distance, declining to swear fealty to him and showing a determination to maintain control of ecclesiastical appointments. He did permit the introduction of a dual system of courts, lay and clerical, which was to cause severe problems in the future, but this was common practice elsewhere in Europe. Though William was sympathetic to Gregory VII and the reformers, English bishops were his tenants-in-chief as much as lay barons were, and, supported by Archbishop Lanfranc, he intended to keep them under royal control. Under his son and successor William II (1087–1100), relations with Rome were less harmonious. The king aroused indignation by keeping bishoprics vacant while he pocketed their revenue; even the see of Canterbury remained unoccupied for four years and was only filled when the king, fearing that he was going to die, was overcome by a sudden (and temporary) fit of piety.

Combining the powers of traditional Anglo-Saxon monarchy with the powers of a Norman feudal overlord, William I was in an immensely strong position. But success for him, as for other medieval kings, largely depended on personal qualities, and in character William was not lacking. He was tough and unyielding, though not

Ely Cathedral, built on what was once an island in the Fens, was begun in 1083, on the site of an older building. It retains an unusually large amount of Norman work.

cruel by the standards of the time. Poachers in his precious forests were mutilated horribly but not executed; even rebels like Hereward the Wake were pardoned. But beyond that, William possessed the two most vital qualifications for a medieval king—skill in administration and success in war. Moreover, the two sons who succeeded him measured up to him reasonably well, though William II's reputation has suffered permanent damage as a result of his alienation of the clergy—who were also the chroniclers.

As often happened on the removal of a strong man, the death of William I in 1087 was followed by chaos as every baron strove to improve his own lot. The chief source of the trouble was Normandy, where Duke Robert, who fulfilled his father's worst expectations, showed no talent for controlling his barons. In England William II, called Rufus ("red"), was beset by rebels who espoused the cause of his undesirable brother. The separate succession in England and Normandy seemed thoroughly impracticable (many barons held land in both countries) and was not accepted on either side of the English Channel.

The hard-swearing, violent Rufus dealt capably with his many enemies. Besides his campaigns in France, which paved the way for the recovery of Normandy, he demolished rebellious barons in England, regained Cumbria (north-west England) from the Scots and mastered much of South Wales. He died in 1100 in a mysterious hunting accident in the New Forest (no motive for murder can be established, and although the man who fired the fatal arrow made haste to leave the kingdom, that would seem to be a sensible precaution in any case).

Henry I completed the conquest of

Below left: Bath Abbey. The Normans built a vast minster here, but it was destroyed by fire in 1137 and rebuilt virtually from scratch.

A 13th-century map of Britain, showing a number of familiar features, including the Roman walls in the north and many towns and counties. It is clear, however, that the cartographer was not a Scotsman.

Normandy, though he spent a large part of his reign (1100–35) suppressing a revolt and fighting his overlord, Louis VI of France, who upheld the cause of Duke Robert's heir, William the Clito.

A rather cold, hard man, Henry proved an able diplomat as well as an energetic general. Relations with the Church, then at the height of its reforming zeal, were sensitive, but Henry handled them well. He reached agreement with Archbishop Anselm, who had been driven into exile by William Rufus because of his support for Rome over the vexed question of investitures, though the king had to give ground in order to reach a compromise. Bishops were to be elected in the king's presence and were to do homage to him before consecration, but the Pope's right of investiture was conceded. In practice, however, the appointment of bishops generally remained with the king.

Henry's continental alliances were to have far-reaching results. In 1120 his son and heir was drowned in the White Ship, a disaster which deeply afflicted the king and left the succession dangerously open. His daughter Matilda, whose first husband had been the Emperor Henry V (an alliance that helped to preserve Normandy) was married to Geoffrey Plantagenet, count of Anjou. Their son, the future Henry II, was born less than two years before the death of the king.

Henry I designated his daughter, Matilda, as his successor, and compelled the barons to swear fealty to her. In fact he did this twice, signifying his fear that the barons would not accept a woman as a ruler, especially a woman married to the young and vigorous Angevin, the traditional enemy of landholders in northern France.

Henry's misgivings were justified.

When he died, Stephen de Blois, his nephew and the eldest grandson of the Conqueror, was promptly accepted as king by the Church, the city of London and most of the court. But Stephen's position was precarious and he was forced to dissipate some of the centralized state controls of his uncle by concessions on investitures, city privileges, the forest laws (always one of the most hated aspects of Norman rule) and other matters. None of this helped when it came to dealing with enemies farther afield: the Welsh ran riot, the

Scots descended deep into England, the Angevins overran Normandy. Stephen's evident weakness had the usual result of sowing doubt, despondency and finally treachery among his own supporters. England gradually succumbed to anarchy, and in 1139 Stephen's rival claimant, Matilda, landed with an army commanded by Robert of Gloucester, a bastard son of Henry I.

The reign of Stephen, nearly twenty years (1135–54) of bad government, or lack of government, was a miserable period. There was very little serious fighting, and the civil war did have its romantic episodes—notably when Matilda, besieged in Oxford at Christmas time, ascaped by a rope from a window and ran off across the snow dressed (so popular legend insists) in her nightgown. But the plight of ordinary people—murdered, plundered, raped and tortured by warring barons, foreign mercenaries, and bands of semiorganized brigands—was dreadful. The horror expressed by the monastic chroniclers cannot be entirely banished by the judgment of modern historians that the state of anarchy was greatly exaggerated. However, it is true that monasticism flourished and that in large areas law and order were maintained by local lords as effectively as in the reign of Henry I, while in the southeast, Stephen's control was not seriously threatened. It is significant too that some of the legal reforms previously credited to Henry II have been traced back to the later, more peaceful, years of Stephen.

What eventually brought about a settlement of the dispute was the fortuitous death of various combatants and the rising Angevin power on the continent, which made barons with French estates hesitate. Geoffrey of Anjou had died in 1151, leaving to his son Normandy, Maine and Anjou. This considerable inheritance was threatened by the enmity of Louis VII of France, whose sister was married to Stephen's son, but in 1152 Louis made a deplorable political blunder. He divorced his wife Eleanor. This lady had many remarkable qualities, but in the immediate circumstances her most notable asset was her possession of the duchy of Aquitaine in her own right. Within weeks Henry married her, and thus gained the whole of western France from Picardy to the Pyrenees.

The death of Stephen's son the following year made the final agreement possible: Stephen kept the throne but acknowledged Henry as his heir. Not long afterwards he died himself, and Henry II came into possession of the largest European empire that any king of England (except, very briefly, Henry V) ever held.

Canterbury Cathedral, headquarters of the Church of England since the time of St Augustine, and scene of a famous martyrdom in the reign of Henry II.

4 Law and Order 1154-1327

The great advances in law and administration during the 12th century were not the inventions of King Henry II; but Henry, whose fierce energy imposed a greater degree of peace and stability on his kingdom, provided the environment in which they could take firm root.

Today we would speak of "reforms" in government and the judicial system, but reform is a modern notion that would have been entirely alien to people of the 12th century. In the Middle Ages, "law" meant "custom"; no one spoke of change, only of restoration: events that appear to us as sharp breaks with traditions were explained as attempts to re-establish old rights which had been eroded by bad practice. Thus, the Constitutions of Clarendon (1165) which laid down the relations between Church and State and provoked the breach between the king and his archbishop, were described by Henry as a statement of the customs existing in the time of Henry I. Magna Carta (1215), which later ages regarded as the charter of English civil liberties, was similarly intended as a reaffirmation of customary relations between the king and his subjects.

Henry was no conscious innovator and his justice was largely a matter of energetic application of sound traditions and practical common sense. His servants, such as the royal justices who made their way around the county courts on indifferent roads and in all weathers, often received their instructions by word of mouth. No book on English common law was written until the mid 13th century, and even that was more concerned with day-to-day problems than legal principles. In spite of the growing influence of canon law, the basis of English law remained English custom: there is plenty of evidence of medieval Englishmen harking back to pre-Norman times in defence of their rights.

Besides expanding the work of itinerant justices, Henry established permanent courts of justice at Westminster (thus ensuring London's place as the English capital). This was chiefly a matter of convenience, as the royal court was so peripatetic an institution: Henry seldom spent more than a few months in one place. The central government remained virtually synonymous with the royal household, though the Exchequer, which was concerned with administration as well as revenue, had been established at Winchester since the reign of Henry I.

The use of juries, the best-remembered aspect of judicial and administrative progress in the reign of Henry II, was, again, nothing new. The data gathered by William I's agents when Domesday Book was being compiled were provided by juries—local representatives who knew the customs of the district. Juries in this sense had been used in Saxon times. In criminal cases, juries were not required to make subtle judgments about evidence, they were only expected to employ their local knowledge of (for example) the character of the accused. In cases of doubt, the accused had to undergo some physical ordeal, often potentially

The fame of Becket spread far and wide; this wall painting commemorating his martyrdom comes from Italy.

lethal, and his guilt or innocence was decided by how well he endured it, the presumption being that God would not allow the guilty to escape unscathed. Henry disliked the system of trial by ordeal or by battle, perhaps as a result of his upbringing in France, where it had been criticised much earlier. He therefore encouraged the use of juries in deciding the actual rights and wrongs of a case. Within a few generations, trial by jury was being claimed as a right.

It was inevitable that the expansion of royal authority and the centralization of government would bring the monarchy into conflict with the other powers in the country—the Church and the feudal aristocracy. From neither contest did the Crown emerge wholly triumphant.

Henry II was anxious to regain the control over the English Church that had been squandered in the reign of Stephen. To that end he made his friend and chancellor, Thomas Becket, archbishop of Canterbury in 1162.

But to the king's disgust, the worldly ex-chancellor, chameleon-like, suddenly turned himself into an ascetic divine, adopted a monk's habit and a hair shirt, and became a fanatical champion of the rights of the clergy, more rigid than the Pope himself.

The dispute which brought the two men into open antagonism concerned the punishment of criminal priests. Henry conceded that a priest accused of a crime should be tried in the Church courts, but he insisted that if he were found guilty, he should be handed over to the royal court for punishment, since the punishments inflicted by the Church courts were usually trivial. Becket refused to give way on this or any other point of conflict. The Pope and the English bishops, while deploring Becket's fanaticism, felt bound to support him and hoped that, when Becket swept out of the kingdom in 1165, some compromise could be patched up. But exile did not soften Becket's zeal, while Henry made reconciliation more difficult by

vindictively persecuting the archbishop's family.

After more than five years, a fragile truce was arranged and Becket returned to England. He at once excommunicated the bishops who had co-operated with the king during his absence and preached a Christmas-day sermon of relentless denunciation from his pulpit in Canterbury cathedral. When Henry heard the news in Normandy, he broke into a fury and demanded to know why no one would rid him of "this low-born priest". Taking him at his word, four knights crossed the Channel, rode swiftly to Canterbury, and cut down the unresisting Becket an the altar steps.

Not for the first time Henry had allowed his notoriously violent temper to get the better of him. But Becket's martyrdom reawakened his keen political acumen. The murdered archbishop at once became England's most popular saint: miracles were being reported from Canterbury almost before his bones were cold. Alive to this development, Henry personally embraced the burgeoning cult, walked barefoot to the tomb, and had himself flogged by the Canterbury monks. Although these signs of repentance averted the fiercest hostility of the Church, on several points the king was forced to give way to Rome. In particular, he allowed that criminal priests should be punished exclusively by the Church courts. By his death, Becket had won the last round.

Later monarchs struggled with mixed success against ecclesiastical privilege. Under Edward I three archbishops were appointed against the king's wishes and one of them, following papal orders, withheld payment of taxes by the Church, which provoked Edward into declaring the clergy outlaws.

Although it is tempting to postulate as a central theme in the political history of medieval England a contest between the Crown and the barons, fundamentally they were not opponents, at least as long as royal government was reasonably strong and efficient. The most serious troubles occurred only when the Crown was weak or in dispute. Thus royal justice as dispensed by Henry II was popular not only with lesser folk but with the barons too, in spite of the fact that it inevitably undermined the rights the barons exercised in the feudal courts.

The successive rebellions which shook and finally shattered the ageing Henry II were largely fomented by his ambitious sons. When his favourite son, John, joined the rebels, Henry at last switched off the dynamic currents that had powered his stocky and aggressive figure from one end of his empire to the other for 35 years without rest, and remarking that he "cared for nothing in the world any more", he turned his face to the wall and died.

The royal law and order that he had established kept England and Normandy reasonably loyal during his own reign and that of his successor, Richard I (1189–99), known as Coeur de Lion, who in ten years spent only a few months in England. Richard gained a glorious reputation as a Crusader, but drained the country to near-bankruptcy to pay for his wars and (after he had allowed himself to be captured by Leopold of Austria) his ransom.

Though he scarcely earned the right to be called the king of England, Richard was a great warrior and, in spite of the wiles of Philippe-August of France, he hung on to his French inheritance. His brother John (1199–1216) was unsuccessful as a soldier and, outmanoeuvred by Philippe, lost a large part of his French lands, including Normandy. This vital difference was enough to make Richard a very popular monarch and John a very unpopular one.

John's reputation as the archetypal "bad king" is hardly fair, but he was certainly an unattractive man and an inadequate and unreliable king. As his brother's governor of Ireland, he had laughed at the old-fashioned appearance of the Irish lords and amused

Below: Robin Hood is a famous English folk-hero—the good man forced into revolt by an evil Establishment, represented in the stories by the Sheriff of Nottingham, where this statue stands, and the representatives of Richard I who was absent, as usual, on crusade.

himself by pulling their long beards. Such behaviour, while possibly suggesting a certain sense of crude fun, was not in the best traditions of royal diplomacy.

John antagonised the English magnates no less surely. Already restless under the increasing weight of royal government and the taxes on property introduced by Richard I's deputies, the English barons objected strongly to the new financial exactions that paid for John's unsuccessful French wars. They resented the king's arbitrary behaviour to individuals (he was suspected of arranging the murder of his nephew, Prince Arthur), and his exclusion from his court of the men who traditionally should have been his closest advisers, i.e. themselves. Faced with near-universal hostility from his politically articulate subjects, John was forced to surrender to their de-

mands in the document later known as Magna Carta (the Great Charter, 1215).

What makes Magna Carta so important is not the document itself so much as the interpretation put upon it later. It was not the great freedom charter that later generations supposed, although it was something more than the result of a political victory by a small class of land-holding magnates intend on securing their feudal rights. It was in fact a hotchpotch of a document, containing clauses that dealt with such matters as fish-traps in the Thames or standard weights and measures. But its important overall effect was to proclaim, both in its individual clauses concerned with specific disputes and in a more general sense, the rule of law—a law which governed the actions of the king no less than the actions of his subjects.

Later, lawyers would find implicit in Magna Carta the principle of no taxation without consent, and the right to trial by jury.

What the Charter did not do was to provide adequate machinery for its enforcement. The king might be constitutionally "under the law", but to keep him there was another matter entirely. John subsequently denied the legality of the Charter on the grounds that he had assented under duress, but he died in 1216, leaving an heir, Henry III (1216–72), only nine years old. The dispute between the Crown and its chief subjects was briefly muted as the barons found themselves responsible for the royal government. But for a hundred years after Magna Carta, and intermittently for three centuries after that, the restraint of royal government remained a recurrent preoccupation of English politics.

Left: Richard the Lion Hearted was taken prisoner by the soldiers of the Holy Roman Emperor in 1192.

Part of the old abbey of Bury St Edmunds, where the barons met to concert opposition to King John before forcing him to sign Magna Carta.

The barons' task was made harder by their own disagreements. Even Henry III, whose political sense was no better developed than his father's, was able to evade baronial control by employing members of his household in the government, and when the barons found a leader of real character in Simon de Montfort, it proved possible to attract a sufficient number of barons to the king's support to defeat Simon at the battle of Evesham (1265).

Simon de Montfort's undoing was brought about not by the king but by his far more capable son, the future Edward I (1272–1307). A powerful figure with a weak eyelid that made him look as though he were on the point of giving a sinister wink, Edward acceded to the throne on his way back from a Crusade. Although posterity was to call him "the English Justinian" (contemporaries called him "Longlegs") his extensive legal reforms were largely conservative, like those of Henry II, and aimed at ending anomalies and reinforcing royal justice. Edward himself was primarily a man of war, and for the expansionist policy he intended to pursue he needed money. Accordingly he set on foot a careful inquiry into royal rights throughout the kingdom, in the manner of William I, refusing to admit the legality of any feudal claims that could not be historically substantiated. Once again the pendulum of power, which had swung over to the barons under the weak rule of Henry III, swung back to the Crown as a strong hand gripped the sceptre.

It was his need for money and his desire to assert royal control that prompted Edward I to summon knights (representatives of the counties) and burgesses (representatives of the towns) to parliament in 1295. This development was not quite the con-

The death of Simon de Montfort at the Battle of Evesham. Deserted by his Welsh levies and strategically outwitted by the forces of the King, he took up his last stand in a circle of his closest supporters and retainers, all of whom died with him.

Below: One of the glories of English medieval architecture, Beverley Minster, in Yorkshire. The west façade, with its twin towers, was not completed until the early 15th century.

defied. When Edward I came to the throne the Welsh prince, Llewelyn ap Gruffyd, held control of virtually the whole country. Llewelyn set himself in fierce opposition to Edward, but failing to carry the whole country with him, he was defeated in 1277. Five years later war broke out again, this time on a national scale. But the result, in spite of the longbow (a Welsh invention), was the same. Llewelyn was killed and his brother David captured and later executed. Edward set about reorganising Wales on the English pattern. As a political gesture, he made his son Prince of Wales in 1301, and the title has been bestowed on the el-

stitutional innovation it appears, and the old name of "Model Parliament" given to this assembly no longer seems appropriate. Knights and burgesses had appeared in a parliament summoned by Simon de Montfort, and John had consulted the knights. Edward wanted them present not to listen to their advice (still less to act on it) but to make sure his wishes were carried out in their districts, and the appearance of the burgesses was merely a sign of the growing prosperity of the towns, encouraged by Edward and other medieval kings as a counterweight to the feudal magnates.

Nevertheless, complaints were made and listened to at Edward's parliament, and by the end of the reign the cry of "redress of grievances before taxation" was to be heard. Moreover, Edward's orders were framed in the form of statutes, not identical with acts of parliament in the modern sense but nevertheless significant: the antecedents of the modern institution can be clearly recognised in the parliament of Edward I.

But these developments had little immediate effect, and certainly the king himself would not have regarded them as very remarkable. Of greater personal interest was his effort to make England a greater kingdom than he found it.

Since Norman times, Celtic Wales had been a chronic danger on England's western flank. Henry II had imposed peace, but since his reign English authority had been frequently

dest son of the monarch from that time ever since.

Scotland proved too tough a nut even for the resolute Edward (the "Hammer of the Scots", as he is described on his tomb) to crack. At first he was content with emphasising his feudal overlordship, but the Scots rebelled, rejected the puppet-king whom Edward had nominated, and formed an alliance with France against England. Edward undertook three punitive expeditions to Scotland and executed the Scots' leader, William Wallace, in 1305. But next year revolt broke out again, under the able leadership of Robert Bruce. On his way to

chastise the Scots once more, Edward died.

The campaign was abandoned by his son Edward II (1307–27), and Robert Bruce, crowned king of Scots, steadily extended his authority over Lowlands and Highlands. Not until the last English-held fortress was besieged by Bruce in 1314 did Edward II himself lead a large army to its relief. At Bannockburn he was utterly routed by Bruce in the greatest victory the Scots ever achieved against the English. Scottish independence was secured until the day, nearly 400 years later, when a peaceful union seemed advantageous to both countries.

The disaster of Bannockburn ruined what little authority Edward II had left over his barons. He was a man unsuited to wear a medieval crown, unbusinesslike and effete. For a period he was almost completely under the control of a baronial council, powerless to take revenge when his favourite, Piers Gaveston, was murdered by his opponents. The rise of a moderate party led, eventually, to an open conflict in which the lords of the north and the Welsh Marches (borders) rose against the king. Edward won the first round thanks to the disunity of his opponents, but in 1326 rebellion broke out again, led by the queen and her lover, Roger Mortimer. Edward was captured, pronounced incompetent, and compelled to abdicate. A few months later he was viciously murdered in Berkeley Castle. His tomb is in Gloucester cathedral.

5 War and Disorder 1327-1471

Nearly every English king since the Conqueror had quarrelled with his French counterpart, who was also his overlord for the lands he held in France. In the reign of Edward III (1327–77) this simmering stew of dispute came to the boil when Edward claimed the throne of France herself. His chief reason for embarking upon this imperialist policy was that war was still the king's business and Edward loved it. But he had more practical reasons, among them French attempts to squeeze him out of his inherited possessions in Gascony and the continuing menace of the Franco-Scottish alliance. He also had a genuine genealogical claim to the French Crown when the death of Charles VI in 1328 left the succession open to question. Not unnaturally, the French preferred the dead king's nephew Philippe VI, the first Valois.

The Hundred Years' War is an inaccurate name for the long contest between France and England which began in 1337, as it lasted more than 100 years and included long periods of peace. Under Edward III and his equally warlike son, the Black Prince, the English were at first very successful. Sluys (1340) was the first great naval victory of the English over the French; Crécy (1346) showed the superiority of modern tactics and well-trained bowmen over the French feudal host; Poitiers (1356) forced the French to surrender large areas of land. But these were mere battles, and the English conquests were short-lived. In the last years of Edward III, when the old king was senile and the

Black Prince dying, France regained nearly all her losses.

The English claim was vigorously revived by Henry V (1413–22), an impressive, almost frightening figure whose early death perhaps prevented English hegemony on a Napoleonic scale. Agincourt (1415) was a remarkable victory against large odds, which enabled Henry to reconquer Normandy and ravage the Ile de France. The French king gave him his daughter to wed and proclaimed him his heir. But Henry died first.

Thereafter the English were forced on to the defensive. The French at last learned to change their military tactics, and a blossoming of nationalist feeling, exemplified in Jeanne d'Arc, proved more formidable than any feudal army. By 1453, the English had

which was consciously French in design). But apart from differences in detail, the basic ideas were the same. Only in the second half of the 14th century did a marked divergence occur. The French Flamboyant style never appeared in England, though it did in pro-French Scotland. Instead, the English evolved the more restrained Perpendicular style, which reached its fullest glory in the elegant fan-vaulting of King's College Chapel, Cambridge.

The effects of the French wars on law and government arose from the king's prolonged absences abroad and his pressing need for money. Finance was a continual problem for royal government even in peaceful times, and it was a problem that was never

lost all their possessions in France except Calais.

The long contest with France naturally affected developments in English (and French) society. Hostility to France encouraged the growth of distinctively English culture. French and Latin were still the tongues of the educated, but English was at last accepted as a literary language. Geoffrey Chaucer, the "father of English literature", took part—and was captured—in the Hundred Years' War (to the King's credit, Edward III ransomed him).

An anti-French cultural reaction could be most easily seen in architectural developments. There were always differences between English and continental styles in architecture. The Saxon, and even the Norman, versions of Romanesque were not identical with their European counterparts, and the great Gothic cathedrals of the 13th century were less formal, less richly decorated, than those of northern France (the contrast is emphasised by Henry III's Westminster Abbey,

fully understood by the king's subjects (the subjects of Charles I no less than the subjects of King John). In the king's absence it was easier to make criticisms and objections, and parliament acquired the habit of attaching political conditions to its assent to new taxes.

Thus parliament assumed a more powerful role. Parliamentary statutes came to have greater weight than royal ordinances, and the "Good Parliament", in reaction against the corruption of royal officials in 1376, managed briefly to impose its own council of advisers on the king. At this time too it became the custom for the Lords and Commons of parliament to meet separately. Not that the Commons wished to take a direct part in government. When Edward III consulted them on his French policy, they declined to give an opinion. That, they said, was a matter for the king and his barons.

The barons themselves gained from the king's absence, and the seeds of future troubles were planted by Edward III when he married his numerous sons to great heiresses, thus creating a small class of territorially powerful, royal-blooded magnates with conflicting ambitions. When his grandson Richard II (1377–99) succeeded to the throne at the age of ten, the royal council was dominated by a few mighty families, mutually hostile.

War in the Middle Ages was a less disruptive social agent than it became in later times, and the Anglo-French contest was not the chief cause of the social turmoil of the 14th century. Religious discontents and the economic changes connected with the decay of feudal relationships and the rise of urban society were more profound influences, and they were linked with a third, more arbitrary and more devastating agent of change—the disease known as plague.

The Black Death—a combination of bubonic and the more deadly pneumonic plague—struck England in 1348. Within two years about one third of the population died. Then it retreated, moving north to devastate the Scots who a year earlier had laughed at England's disaster. Twelve years later plague returned, then again and again, never as fiercely as in 1348

like the priest whose parishioners complained that he muddled Jesus with Judas. Fundamentally, the trouble was that there were too many clergy—priests and monks—for the population to sustain. They were under-employed, and the devil made work for idle hands.

From the prevailing religious controversy emerged the figure of John Wycliff. An ascetic, rather pedantic priest, with many supporters at court, Wycliff did not appear to be the stuff of which popular reformers are made; but when he was arrested in London, the citizens rioted. Although he cannot be called a "Protestant"—he never approached the Lutheran belief in justification by faith—he nevertheless expressed most of the criticisms that were to be made at the time of the Reformation, condemning not only the abuses and corruption of the Church but attacking the doctrine of transubstantiation as "blasphemous folly".

Wycliff's protests against the established eccliastical order had political implications (it is not surprising that he found favour with ruling magnates like John of Gaunt, eager to divert ecclesiastical endowments to their own pockets) and they were also intimately connected with the social discontents caused by the gradual break-up of feudal society.

An intense shortage of labour resulting largely from the plague (although the 14th-century decline in population appears to have set in before the Black Death) hastened the process, already under way, of commutation of labour services (i.e. tenants paying rent instead of providing labour). Wages rocketed, as landlords sought desperately for hands to till their untended fields; many switched to sheep, which required less labour.

but each time killing thousands of people, as well as cattle.

This staggering disaster, widely interpreted as a sign of God's wrath, stimulated discontent and disruption in field and cloister.

The English had never been particularly fond of priests, and in the 14th century the grounds for criticising the clergy were abundant. Ecclesiastical authority in general had suffered grievously from the papal schism, and in the English Church the evils of ab-

senteeism, pluralism, corruption and fraud were everywhere evident. The people of one diocese remarked with cynical humour that their bishop was like the strawberries: he came but once a year and stayed not long. Of course there were good and honest priests: Chaucer describes one in his *Canterbury Tales* (though his other clerical characters are an unsavoury lot), and probably there were many like him. Many others, no doubt, were simply not very capable, or plain ignorant,

The government strove to control wage inflation by a succession of statutes, but their efforts failed, as the laws were widely ignored and served only to irritate the wage-earners. (All this has a familiar ring to anyone living in Britain in the 1970s).

Events were outrunning the capacity of the established system to control them, and not only in the countryside. In the towns, the craft guilds warred constantly with the town government and with each other. Some of the con-temporary attacks on privilege have a startling, if misleadingly, modern sound. In Oxford, peasants carrying a black flag marched on the university. A radical priest, John Ball, rhetorically inquired who had been the "gentleman" when Adam was cultivating the Garden of Eden. The poet William Langland, in his *Piers Plowman*, passionately exalted the figure of the ploughman while condemning corruption in high places. The inimitable Chaucer portrayed his group of Can-terbury pilgrims in a troubled, turbulent time, a time when violent change seemed imminent.

But there is little grimness in the *Canterbury Tales*. Chaucer also communicated the vigour of English life, the coarse liveliness, the ambition, and indeed the prosperity of the times. For in spite of discontent and distress, for many people the times were prosperous. In the sheep-rearing districts of East Anglia and the West Country, churches larger than the population required rose above the village roofs, enduring testimony of the profits of the wool trade.

In 1380 the government, hard-pressed by enemies abroad, imposed a heavy poll tax. It was fiercely resented, especially by those who found that heavy taxes did not prevent the French raiding the coasts, and was widely evaded. The government, with the determination of the desperate, sent out well-armed tax collectors in force. Quite suddenly, the country was in revolt.

The Peasants' Revolt of 1381 was at first strongest in the south-east. Its leaders included some firebrands but in general showed an astonishing degree of good sense and determination—qualities not reflected by their chief opponents. The impressive Wat Tyler led the men of Kent on London, and the court took refuge in the Tower, the great palace-fortress begun by William the Conqueror. The rebels were careful to level their complaints at the royal councillors, not at the King, to whom they professed loyalty. The 14-years-old Richard II agreed to most of their demands and showed quick wits and courage when one of his followers, provoked by Wat Tyler, turned and stabbed the rebel leader. Richard promptly spurred his horse towards the rebels and cried that he would be their new leader—a gesture that undoubtedly averted worse bloodshed.

The revolt spread quickly outside London, but largely through the lack of cohesion in the governing class. When a local lord or town government showed determination, they were often able to resist successfully. The revolt died, and although there was no great blood-bath like that which followed the Jacquerie in France, it naturally provoked a reaction by the frightened rulers. The young king's promises were not fulfilled, rebel leaders were executed and reformers, including Wycliff's followers, the Lollards, were suppressed.

Richard II, a gifted but unreliable man with a trace of megalomania, at last succeeded in freeing himself from the suffocating control of the contending magnates, most of them his uncles. But though he reasserted royal authority, he lacked the persistence to

maintain it and, foreshadowing the mistake of Charles I, he showed a disturbing tendency to regard his own person as the sole fount of law. Having expelled his cousin Henry of Lancaster (son of John of Gaunt) from the country for a ten-years period, he waited until Henry was out of the way and then declared his exile permanent and seized the Lancastrian estates. Henry returned to England with an army, took the king by surprise, and captured him. Finding himself without substantial support and a prisoner to boot, Richard agreed to abdicate in Henry's favour. He was later assassinated. These events foreshadowed civil war two generations later.

Henry IV (1399–1413) wore the crown that he had usurped uneasily. He found the great magnates no less troublesome, and he was handicapped by the political debts that he owed to many of them. As far as possible, however, he clung to the rights of the Crown, and at least succeeded in passing it safely to his son Henry V (1413–22). The second Lancastrian king had ambitions that ran far beyond the borders of England (he once spoke of knocking on the doors of Jerusalem), but his plans were foiled by his death at the age of 35.

His son Henry VI (1422–61) acceded to the throne at the age of nine months and grew up to be a gentle, likeable man, with a tenuous grasp of reality. The ruling-class bickering, endemic since the death of Edward III, slowly degenerated into civil war.

Civil war is always a highly emotive subject, and the Wars of the Roses have been more romanticised than most. It is hardly accurate to call them a civil war at all; they were little more than a family feud, fought out by armed retainers. The armies involved were very small, major battles were few, and no expensive sieges were undertaken. Indeed, the economic effect on the country at large was slight. Though brief depressions in the cloth trade can be related to military events, townsmen could virtually ignore the Wars of the Roses.

That romantic name is also false, a later invention referring to the red rose sometimes worn as an emblem by supporters of the House of Lancaster and the white rose worn by supporters of

the House of York. In 1455, when the armed conflict began, the Lancastrians held possession of the throne in the not very satisfactory person of Henry VI. The Yorkist leaders were the duke of York (direct descendant of another of Edward III's sons) and his son, who became Edward IV (1461–83).

The accession of Edward and the Yorkist victory at Towton, fought in a snowstorm, did not conclude the episode, for Edward lost the throne briefly in 1470–71, when Henry VI made a brief reappearance before being put away again and (probably) murdered. Strictly, the last battle of the Wars of the Roses was the battle of Bosworth in 1485, which brought an entirely new dynasty to the English throne in the person of Henry VII, first of the Tudors.

London in the late Middle Ages was becoming a substantial city. London Bridge, visible in the background of this miniature, was a source of great pride to the citizens, who regarded it, perhaps justly, as one of the Wonders of the World.

6 Foundation of the Modern State 1471-1603

The Wars of the Roses were an antique play performed on centre stage while more important activities were taking place in the wings. Central authority was collapsing at the very time when strong central government was most needed. Contemporaries recognised this: there were constant complaints of corrupt administration and disruption of trade. The men of Kent, under John Cade, again marched on London (1450) with a formidable list of grievances against the government; Londoners rioted against the privileges of foreign merchants; ambitious nobles grabbed land by force or intimidation; trade and piracy were often indistinguishable. But the widespread feeling of discontent with the anarchy of the times could be harnessed by a strong government seeking to establish the central control that was needed.

The foundations of the modern nation-state that sprang into vigorous life under the Tudor dynasty were laid in the period after 1471, the year that Edward IV made his throne secure by killing the great earl of Warwick, the "King-maker", at the battle of Barnet. A large, likeable and intelligent man, Edward had most of the qualities needed for strong kingship—except that of longevity, for he died at forty, worn out, it is said, by over-indulgence in the lusts of the flesh. He stopped one enervating drain on the nation's energies by bringing to an end, after one brief flourish of arms, the futile war with France. He won the approval of the increasingly important commercial class by putting the royal revenue on a sound footing. Not all the methods he employed were popular, still less ethical, but the estates he confiscated were those of his enemies, and the forced loans and gifts he extracted were paid without too much protest. Few laymen complained when he taxed the clergy, nor when he attacked ecclesiastical privileges and the Church courts. The merchants were especially favoured by a king who was, in a private capacity, a considerable merchant himself, carrying on a lucrative trade in Italian fancy goods. The wool and cloth trades, already expanding in periods of peace, reached record heights by about 1480. Population was rising, and the long period of agricultural depression, which with ups and downs dated back to the mid 14th century, steadily receded.

Looking back, the great potential of England in the late 15th century is clearly apparent, though it was hidden from contemporaries. To all appearances, England was still a country on the fringe of the civilized world, a place of small account. The Atlantic sea routes which would bring England from the fringe to the centre of European affairs, were undiscovered. Strong sinews of trade connected England with the Low Countries, the Baltic and the Mediterranean, but England's vast productive capacity was still dormant. English shipping was known on most European coasts, but her naval might was still asleep, though gently stirring as Edward IV harried pirates in the English Channel.

Towards the end of Edward's reign his brother Richard played the most prominent part in government, and when Edward died Richard gained control of the council. The boy-king Edward V and his younger brother disappeared, and it was later announced that they had died. Richard III (1483–85) was crowned king. The

fate of the missing princes presents the most popular puzzle in English history. Richard has a small but passionate group of admirers who deny that he was responsible for the murder of his nephews and, on stronger grounds, condemn Shakespeare's sinister portrait of him as mere Tudor propaganda. However, Richard III had other enemies besides dynastic rivals, and he lacked the attractive personality of his brother.

The death of his own son in 1484 weakened Richard's position by once more throwing open the question of the succession, and although the direct Lancastrian line was extinct, another claimant appeared in Henry, duke of Richmond, a member of the Welsh house of Tudor, who was descended from John of Gaunt through his mother. Henry Tudor promised to wed a Yorkist princess, and thus

gained the support of Yorkists antagonized by Richard III. In August, 1485, he landed in Wales and marched towards the English Midlands. Richard met him at Bosworth. As the battle began, some of Richard's supporters treacherously changed sides according to a prearranged plan. Richard was killed and the crown, which he had worn into battle, rolled under a bush. When the fighting ended, someone found it there and placed it on the head of Henry Tudor.

Henry VII (1485–1509), "our current sovereign lord", as parliament rather cynically proclaimed him, inherited a throne more secure than it looked. Though rebellions were raised against him, Henry was able to treat his opponents with such disdain that one of the "Pretenders" was put to work washing dishes in the royal kitchens. That such rebellions failed to

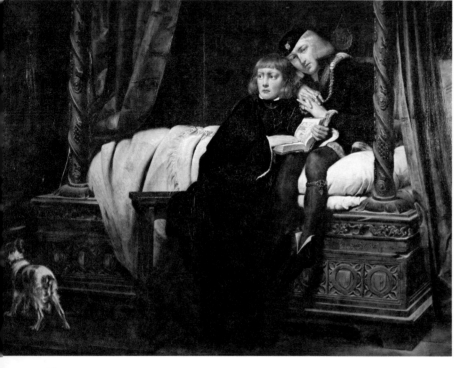

hainrich · von · gottes ·
genaden kuing · von ·
· engelland vnd · zu ·
frankrich her · zu ·
irlanten

Left: Henry VII, following policies adopted by Edward IV, recognised the advantages of peaceful trade, over the glory of conquest.
Below: By marrying a Yorkist princess, Henry hoped to prevent a renewal of dynastic rivalry.

shake the Tudor throne was largely due to the disarray and impoverishment of the nobility. Like Edward IV, Henry gobbled up the estates of his opponents and as they included all those who had fought for Richard III, the Crown acquired vast new territories. Henry avoided the mistake made by Edward III in creating powerful rivals among his offspring by marrying them astutely into European royal houses, not to native lords. But the most effective aspect of his campaign against too-powerful subjects was the statute of 1487 forbidding the nobles to keep bands of armed and uniformed servants. This was not the first attempt to abolish private armies, but it was the first successful attempt, and was enforced by the prerogative courts, such as the Court of Star Chamber, which was simply a department of the royal council and not susceptible to intimidation by the pow-

erful. The nobility were fast losing predominance in the king's council: Henry's most trusted servants were chiefly clergymen, lawyers, knights and merchants. This tacit alliance between the king and the middle classes against the nobles was an old one, but it gained strength from their common purpose under the early Tudors. In the provinces the justices of the peace, local gentry in charge of administration as well as justice, came to replace the old office of sheriff and the feudal organization of the manor. They proved excellent servants of the Crown and, with more restricted duties, survive to this day.

Henry exploited every possible source of revenue, including various feudal dues that were beginning to look archaic. He trebled the royal revenue in the course of his reign and, like Edward IV, took part privately in international trade. He relaxed duties on

the wool trade and fostered domestic industry. He received a parliamentary grant to fight the French, then accepted a huge payment from the French for not fighting them. His financial exactions were often ruthless, and when Henry VIII (1509–47) came to the throne he at once committed the enormously popular act of executing two of his father's chief tax collectors, a wolfish pair named Empson and Dudley.

Henry VIII, handsome and accomplished, was more popular than his father but a great deal less crafty. Inheriting a safe crown and—desirable rarity—a full treasury, he was spoiled and overconfident. With the connivance of the man who became his chief minister, Thomas Wolsey, son of a prosperous butcher, he insisted on going to war in France, though his exploits there did comparatively little damage to either side. Nevertheless,

Left: Henry VIII had many of the vices and virtues of the typical "bluff Englishman" of popular legend. His political "skill" was largely a matter of instinct and luck.
Below: A splendid non-event—the meeting of two flashy monarchs, Henry VIII and François I, at the Field of the Cloth of Gold in 1520. Then as now, the real diplomacy did not take place at a pageant.

his part in creating a powerful monarchy was no less important than his father's. The reign of Henry VII had been decisive in vanquishing one of the Crown's main rivals—the feudal aristocracy. Henry VIII presided over the destruction of another—perhaps more formidable—rival, the Roman Church.

The immediate cause of Henry VIII's quarrel with the Pope was his desire to take a new wife. Catherine of Aragon had passed childbearing age and her only surviving child was a daughter, Mary. Henry knew well that not the least of the duties of a dynastic monarch was to produce an heir; moreover, he lusted for an English girl, Anne Boleyn. He claimed that his marriage to Catherine of Aragon was wrong because she had previously been married to his elder brother (who had died young). In normal circumstances, a papal annulment might have been easily granted, but when the imperial forces sacked Rome in 1527 the Pope fell under the control of the Emperor Charles V, Catherine's nephew.

Wolsey tried hard to carry out his master's wishes, but Pope Clement VII prevaricated skilfully and Henry grew impatient. At the same time Wolsey's foreign policy, which had consisted in holding the balance between the two great European powers, collapsed in

ruins when the Emperor and François I made peace without bothering to consult England. Wolsey, who had grown so powerful that foreign ambassadors came to see him before the king, fell swiftly and sensationally from his great eminence.

There was nothing new in a king of England challenging papal authority. The first act of the Reformation parliament was directed against the long-standing inconvenience of the Church courts, and in attacking clerical abuses Henry was able to invoke a statute of the late 14th century. But this time the royal challenge was carried through to its logical conclusion: the total abolition of papal authority in England and the installation of the king as supreme head of the Church.

This constitutional revolution would have been impossible but for the strength of the reform movement in England. Lollardy, though suppressed, had never died since Wycliff's time; anticlericalism had been stimulated by the extreme unpopularity of Wolsey; and Luther's proclamations had found many sympathisers in England, especially at Cambridge university. There was no doubt that Henry carried pupular feeling with him when he made the break with Rome, although a few great men like Thomas More and John Fisher preferred to die as "traitors" than ak-

drafted, "is an empire"—meaning an autonomous state with no allegiances beyond its borders.

In the long run, what was done in the English Reformation was not more important than how it was done. It was carried out by acts of parliament, thus confirming the principle that the highest authority in the kingdom was the king in parliament. In the previous reign of 23 years, the king had met parliament only six times; the Reformation parliament summoned by Henry VIII in 1529 was not dissolved until 1535.

If the motives for the Reformation were chiefly political, beneficial financial results also accrued. Henry VIII had soon spent his father's treasure and ecclesiastical property provided a welcome infusion. The combined income of the English monasteries was not far short of the total revenue of the Crown: an irresistible lure. Monks were not popular figures on the whole, and the ruling class, foreseeing cheap sales of land, eagerly supported the at-

tack on their foundations. Cromwell's men carried out visitations and reported corruption, idleness and vice, as they were intended to do (though many of their charges were fair enough). Between 1536 and 1539 the monasteries were dissolved. They yielded vast treasure, but much of it was creamed off by crafty courtiers, and the royal treasury was soon empty again.

The destruction of the monasteries undoubtedly caused some social distress. It was one of the causes of a rebellion in the north of England, known as the Pilgrimage of Grace, which broke out in 1536. So numerous were the "pilgrims" that Henry's general, the duke of Norfolk, hesitated to engage them, but the rebellion was crushed by the customary means—fair promises to make the rebels disperse followed by execution of their leaders.

Although several Protestants, as well as Catholics, were burned in the 1540s, in his last years Henry VIII

knowledge Henry's supremacy in the Church.

Henry's revolution was political and constitutional; he sought no change in doctrine. After all, he had earned from the Pope the title *Fidei Defensor* for his confutation of Luther not many years before. But having embraced reform, Henry—and the country—were inevitably carried some way along the road followed by the Reformers. The king's chief agent in carrying out the Reformation was Thomas Cromwell, son of a blacksmith and an administrator of genius, who was not concerned with questions of faith in themselves. Cromwell was the apostle of the nation-state. "This realm", declared the vital act banning appeals to Rome, which Cromwell

seemed to be moving towards the new religion. At any rate, he appointed Protestants as guardians of Edward VI (1547–53), his only son by his third wife, Jane Seymour. (Henry had three more wives after Jane but no more children). Under the two Lord Protectors, the dukes of Somerset (1547–49) and Northumberland (1549–53), a thorough doctrinal change was carried out. The first English Prayer Book (1549) included a modified form of the Mass, but the second (1552), much influenced by Zwingli, abjured all "Romish" ritual and banished words like "priest" and "altar".

But Edward's death at sixteen brought to the throne Mary (1553–58), daughter of Catherine of Aragon and a devout Roman Catholic. She was determined to put back the clock, restoring not only the old religion but papal authority as well. Her marriage to Philip II of Spain strengthened her in this resolve, though Philip brought little comfort and no heir to this sad and pathetic queen. What ruined Mary's cause was her enforcement of the laws against heresy and the burning of about 300 Protestants. That was persecution on a small scale compared with many other countries, but it earned the queen the name "Bloody Mary" and, together with the unpopular Spanish marriage, lost her much popular sympathy.

Mary's sister Elizabeth (1558–1603) was the daughter of

The Tudor parliament in session. Although Henry VIII had raised the prestige of parliament during the Reformation, it was still the King's (or at this time, the Queen's) instrument.

Henry VIII and Anne Boleyn and thus, as she liked to boast, thoroughly English. She was perhaps the most brilliant politician who ever sat on the English throne: she made even her virginity a diplomatic weapon worth a fleet of warships. It was the task of Elizabeth and her able ministers to settle the problem of a religion once and for all. The pendulum had swung violently from right to left and back again: to bring it to a peaceful stop, a central position was required. Elizabeth herself, who had no very deep religious feelings, favoured the status quo of Henry VIII's reign, Catholicism without Rome, but the final settlement was pushed farther to the left by the pressure of Calvinist exiles who came flooding back after Mary's death.

In view of the fierce feelings that religious controversy aroused in the 16th century, it was a highly successful settlement, having lasted to the present day. On particularly sensitive points of doctrine or ritual, it was deliberately ambiguous, allowing for the considerable divergence of views that the Church of England has always managed to enfold. For example, the Queen was described not as Supreme Head of the Church but Supreme Governor—implying a denial of any priestly function but otherwise ambiguous. The settlement was, in fact, a political masterpiece of a characteristically English kind, sacrificing precision, even principle, for the sake of avoiding trouble. It was widely accepted by a people wearied of the recent changes; it was strengthened by the growing hostility to Spain and by the skilful administration of Elizabethan bishops like Matthew Parker and John Whitgift; and it received political justification in the splendid prose of Hooker's *Ecclesiastical Polity* (1593).

Memorials of Francis Drake are kept at Buckland Abbey, which he bought with the profits of his voyage around the world.
Below: The Queen, attended by gallants of the court, being conveyed to Blackfriars on a litter.

Henry VIII's aggressive nature, only partly checked by Wolsey in the first half of his reign, meant an end of the policy of avoiding war which his father had followed. Wales was easily mastered and Henry declared himself king of Ireland, the first English king to take that title, but though he tried to force the Reformation on the Irish, they remained loyal to the Pope.

The revival of the French wars as usual lured the Scots over the border, but they were defeated with terrible slaughter at Flodden (1513). Later, Henry raised the English kings' claim to the Scottish throne, and war was renewed in the 1540s. The Scots were willing to marry their infant queen Mary to the future Edward VI, but they boggled at Henry's conditions, and the burning of Edinburgh hardly

Charming, courageous and far from stupid, Mary Queen of Scots had that common failing of Renaissance princes, over-confidence, which perverted her political judgment.

encouraged a policy of peaceful union. Finally, the angry Scots revived the "old alliance" by sending Mary to France where she later married the Dauphin.

The Franco-Scottish pact was countered by the marriage of Mary Tudor to Philip II of Spain, though the Spanish marriage ultimately led Mary into a grimly paradoxical war against the Pope, who was trying to eject the Spaniards from Naples. Calais, the last English possession in France, was lost in 1558, to Mary's grief. She said that when she died, as she soon did, the name of Calais would be found engraved on her heart.

Elizabeth, and the wisest of her councillors, wanted "to teach still peace to grow". Like her grandfather, she regarded war as ruinously expensive, besides being morally undesirable (though tough, Elizabeth was humane). But she found it was even more difficult to avoid war than to avoid marriage; many of her subjects frequently clamoured for both. As with her many suitors, so with foreign powers she adopted a policy of hesitation and confusion, which sometimes degenerated into downright deceit. She did intervene strongly against the French/Catholic party in Scotland, but one unfortunate by-product of the subsequent victory of the Protestant/ Nationalist party was that Mary Queen of Scots, who had returned to reign in Scotland after the death of François II, was rejected by her subjects and sought refuge in England in 1568. Like Elizabeth, Mary of Scots was a granddaughter of Henry VII, and in Rome and Madrid she was acclaimed as rightful queen of England. For ten years she was the centre of plots and conspiracies. In the end, Elizabeth reluctantly consented to her royal cousin's execution.

By that time England's most dangerous enemies were no longer the Scots and the French, but the Spaniards. Henry VII had signed a long lasting treaty with Spain, and Philip II had married Mary Tudor. He offered to marry Elizabeth after Mary's death, and though politely rejected, he remained for a time friendly towards England, until the interests of the two countries drifted into opposition.

Under Philip II Spain was becoming the spearhead of the Counter-Reformation, while England was the most substantial Protestant state. More particularly, a clash occurred over the Netherlands, so vital a country for

56

Elizabeth, last and greatest of the Tudors, a born ruler if ever there was one. During the reign of her elder sister she, as a young girl, had stood in the same danger as Mary Queen of Scots did in her own reign, but she handled affairs more capably.

English trade and security, where the Dutch rose against Spanish rule. But the chief area of Anglo-Spanish conflict was the New World. The English had never accepted the presumptuous division of the world into Spanish and Portuguese hemispheres, which was sanctified by Rome in the Treaty of Tordesillas (1494). In any case, the North American mainland had been discovered by John Cabot (an Italian in English service) before Columbus had progressed beyond the West Indies, although the English, unlike the Spaniards, had not followed up that first discovery. But in the 1560s John Hawkins challenged the Spanish monopoly by transporting Africans to sell as slaves to conniving Spanish colonists. On his third voyage, on which Francis Drake captained one of the ships, Hawkins was caught by a Spanish fleet and badly mauled. This attack, carried out under a truce, confirmed in the fiercely Protestant Drake an almost pathological hatred of Spain, a hatred that many of his countrymen shared. In the 1570s Drake and other English "sea dogs" constantly raided Spanish ships and colonies in the Caribbean area. Drake's famous voyage around the world (1577–80) was merely the corollary of his attack on the hitherto unmolested Spanish settlements on the Pacific coast of the Americas. Elizabeth's government disclaimed responsibility for these raids but secretly took shares in the profits, and when Drake reached home in 1580 Elizabeth knighted him on the deck of his ship. Meanwhile, England searched for allies: the desire for French support explains the on-off engagement of Elizabeth to the duke of Anjou, the most grotesque of her many abortive courtships.

Events came to a head in 1585. The Dutch leader William the Silent had been killed and the duke of Parma was overrunning the temporarily demoralized Dutch; the last of the Valois kings was too effete to be of any assistance. Spanish troops landed in Ireland and the Catholic Guise party seemed to be rising again in Scotland while at home Secretary of State Walsingham unearthed a succession of plots against Elizabeth. The Queen steeled herself to do what she had so long evaded; she sent an army to help the Dutch. At the same time Drake sacked Spanish ports, crossed the Atlantic, and captured the major towns of San Domingo and Cartagena. The Netherlands expedition accomplished

57

Left: The execution of Mary Queen of Scots was long delayed but perhaps inevitable. Even if she had behaved more judiciously, she still represented a constant threat to Elizabeth.

little, though it did briefly check Parma at Zutphen, where Sir Philip Sydney, the finest flower of Elizabeth's dazzling court, was killed. But Philip II resolved that England must be crushed.

The "invincible" armada was supposed to set out in 1587, but Drake's daring raid on Cadiz ("singeing the king of Spain's beard", as he put it) delayed it for twelve months. The following year Elizabeth, once more nursing hope of avoiding war, kept Drake at home and the armada sailed. Consisting of about 130 ships, it was planned to embark Parma's army and transport it to England, but the whole expedition was clumsy both in conception and execution. Though the Spanish ships were too powerful to be sunk by straight-forward gunnery, the battle that lasted sporadically for nine days in the Channel was striking proof of the superiority of English ships and seamen. Parma's men were never embarked, and less than half the Spanish fleet reached home safely.

The defeat of the armada was only the beginning of a war that lasted until 1604. England, which had no regular army, remained on the defensive except in the West Indies, and there improved Spanish defences prevented Drake and his comrades repeating their earlier successes. There were further Spanish attempts at invasion, and a few troops did manage to land in Cornwall. But in the Netherlands, the Dutch made their independence secure.

Although later generations looked back at the reign of Elizabeth as a time of blissful peace and stability, it was a period of profound social change and disturbance. The seeds of the troubles of the 17th century were already sprouting in the 16th.

Economic enterprise was increasing. Trade routes were opened to Russia and the Levant, and a sea route to the Far East was eagerly though unsuccessfully sought. Coal was mined on a much greater scale and provided extra income for new landowners on the confiscated monastic estates. Farming was more businesslike, and profit-conscious landowners erected fences on the old open fields to enclose their sheep. This enclosure of land was the chief source of agrarian protest (writers on agriculture spoke of sheep as though they were man-eating tigers), and although statistically minded social historians have asserted that the extent of enclosure was much exaggerated, it certainly contributed to the dangerous problem of unemployment. Roving bands of unemployed were a constant source of anxiety to Elizabethans, like bomb-planting dissidents in our own time. Agrarian discontent sometimes rose to the pitch of revolt, as in Robert Kett's rebellion in Norfolk in 1549, when some 3,000 peasants were killed by the mercenaries hired to suppress them.

Tudor governments were compelled to recognise the need for the state to interfere in matters of social welfare. The Statute of Labourers and Apprentices (1563) attempted to regulate and enforce apprenticeship and even to fix local wage rates. The measures culminating in the Poor Law of 1601, which formed the basis of state welfare until the 19th century, set up a system of local administration, supported by taxation, to deal with the problem of the destitute. Such measures may have been rudimentary and inhumane by

Below: The English victory over the Spanish Armada in 1588 really owed as much to the Spaniards' poor organization and bad luck to the superiority of English ships and men.

Bottom: The persecution of Roman Catholic priests in the 16th century is still an emotive subject. To the English government they were all traitors, but the Queen's insistence that no one was condemned for their beliefs alone rings rather hollow.

The Bradford table carpet shows scenes of rural life in the reign of Elizabeth I.

modern standards, but they represented a great advance in national welfare. They were not echoed by any other contemporary European government, and the Poor Law system probably worked better in the early 17th century than it did at any time in the 18th.

Nevertheless, it did not work very well. Tudor governments had no regular police or army (a fact which makes nonsense of the assertion that Tudor England was a kind of police state: the Elizabethan justice of the peace was not a political commissar). But the result was that laws were often more honoured in the breach than the observance.

More socially disruptive than enclosures was the steep inflation of prices in 16th-century Europe, caused by the torrent of American silver pouring into Spain and aggravated in England by Henry VIII's debasement of the coinage (corrected by a reissue under Elizabeth). The price rise had a marked effect on the fortunes of the landowning aristocracy. Exactly what was happening in the 16th- and early 17th-century "crisis of the aristocracy" is still a matter for argument among historians, but a basic conflict between feudalism and capitalism, in many different aspects, was the cause of sharply shifting fortunes in wealth and property.

On the whole, the standard of living was rising quite fast. People whose fathers had eaten off wooden plates and slept on wool and horsehair now supped off pewter and slept on linen and goose-down, smoked tobacco, and ate new foods like potatoes. Both tobacco and potatoes came from Virginia, and the former at least was made fashionable by Sir Walter Raleigh, the "dark star" of Elizabeth's court whose attempts to found the first Virginia colony ended in failure.

Part of the attraction of the Elizabethan age lies in its sheer vitality and exuberance—sometimes, as in the coarse pursuit of quick fortunes, a vulgar exuberance, but characteristically expressed in more attractive forms. It was the first great age of the English country house, and gentlemen who at an earlier time would have built churches for the glory of the Virgin Mary built mansions for the en-

Late 16th-century England produced an astonishing gallery of glittering talents—and one glorious, immortal genius, William Shakespeare.

tertainment of the Virgin Queen. The grafting of Classical and Italian styles on the English Gothic tradition was carried out with great success, and houses like Longleat, Wollaton or the long-vanished Nonsuch palace (begun by Henry VIII) achieved real grandeur.

The mixture of medieval and modern, of superstition and worldliness, adds to the fascination of the age. A great geographical project like Martin Frobisher's search for the North-West Passage was turned on the flimsiest evidence into a great rush for gold, which still attracted investment from hard-headed merchants long after it should have become obvious to the simplest mind that there was no gold to be had on the distant Canadian

shores. At the same time, ideas were distilling in the mind of the young Shakespeare that remain wholly relevant to us today.

The full flowering of the English Renaissance belongs to the last two decades of the 16th century, when Marlowe and Shakespeare were writing, when Edmund Spenser's *Faery Queen*—a lyrical glorification of the Queen and the age—was published, when the philosopher and scientist Francis Bacon began contemplating the importance of scientific experiment, and when the brief but beautiful life of the English madrigal

was virtually encompassed. The music of Byrd, Tallis and others owed much to the medieval religious tradition, but as music-making became a popular domestic pastime, old themes were transformed for secular purposes. In painting, the Elizabethans had less interest. They liked portraits—chiefly of themselves, and by Flemish artists—but Nicholas Hilliard brought new brilliance to the art of the miniature.

Literature is the greatest glory of the Elizabethan Renaissance. The splendid figure of Shakespeare stands far above all, but if he had never lived the names of his fellow play-wrights—Marlowe, Jonson, Kyd, Greene and several more—might be better known. English as a literary language was still young and growing, and the Elizabethans delighted in expanding its vocabulary and extending its imagery. A letter from a squire's wife to a silversmith, or the chance remarks of the Queen herself, managed to combine the elegance of a caress with the impact of a punch. Every English poet must have sometimes wished he had been born about 1550.

The most remarkable example of Elizabethan prose, the King James Authorized Version of the Bible, was a team effort, published eight years after the Queen's death. Though recently superseded in the Church of England by a new translation in plain, schoolmasterly language, it remains perhaps the finest ornament of English literature.

But the King James Bible has a baroque quality signalling the changing times. When it appeared, new religious and constitutional problems, barely suppressed in Elizabeth's last years, preoccupied the government. The Elizabethan age was already receding into that golden glow, as of sunlight on an autumn evening, from which no revisionist historian nor any earnest, statistically based analysis has quite managed to retrieve it.

Right: A group of Catholic gentry conspired to blow up king and parliament in 1605, but Guy Fawkes was discovered among the gunpowder in the cellars just in time. The conspirators were rounded up and executed in the horrible manner reserved for traitors.
Far right: Elizabeth had always been rather stingy with titles, but James I foolishly handed out honours in great numbers, and thus cheapened royal patronage.

7 Revolution 1603-1689

In her famous last speech to the Commons, Queen Elizabeth told her subjects that she considered it the greatest glory of her reign that she had reigned with their love. Yet in less than forty years, civil war had broken out between Crown and Parliament. How did it happen?

There was no one fundamental cause of the English Civil War, and probably there will never be an explanation that is both simple and convincing. Signs of trouble appeared in Elizabeth's reign. The rise of Puritanism and parliamentary "constitutionalism" presented a threat to the established order which was apparent long before Elizabeth's death, and the economic instability and resulting social disruption of the period were probably greater than they seemed, certainly greater than they seemed to people in the 17th century looking back fondly to Elizabethan peace and stability. There was a strong sense of dissatisfaction and melancholy in late Elizabethan culture. The Elizabethans seemed to be losing faith in their own society: Shakespeare's later plays often took a grim view of human nature,

and contemporary portraits reveal expressions profoundly gloomy. The subject was dissected with a mixture of wit and pedantry by Robert Burton in his *Anatomy of Melancholy* (1621).

Some people have detected a simultaneous decline in taste—a vulgarity apparent in the second-rate dramatic tragedy of the Jacobean period, and in the decorative arts. Such matters are largely subjective, but no one would deny a decline in the quality of political leardership. In his book *The Offshore Islanders* (1972) Paul Johnson prints adjacent pictures of a meeting of Elizabethan ministers—all stately decorum, bare heads, dark gowns and neat ruffs—and a meeting of James I's council twenty years later—lounging, inattentive courtiers in feathered hats and flashy cloaks. It is a striking illustration of degeneration at the top, from the dignity and seriousness of government by Elizabeth and her ministers to the political irresponsibility and frivolity of the Stuart kings and their favourites. (However, the contrast must not be exaggerated. The Earl of Essex, the last of Elizabeth's gallants who was executed for treason

in 1601, was hardly a model of political responsibility, while on the other hand frivolity was not a fault often associated with King Charles I.)

The Elizabethan religious settlement had not satisfied the English Puritans, whose spokesmen in parliament voiced their discontent with Roman ritual retained by the Church of England. They demanded more preaching, condemned the wearing of vestments, and called for the abolition of bishops. This last demand was dangerous and unacceptable, striking directly at the Church-State establishment. James I (1603–25) summed up the implications succinctly: "No bishop, no king". Parliamentary dissent was vociferous enough for Elizabeth to ban all discussion of religious questions, which led to a serious confrontation over the rights of members in 1572. But Elizabeth took a firm line, supported by Archbishop Whitgift and his ecclesiastical court, which operated outside the common law (Burghley, Elizabeth's outstanding minister, compared the court with the Roman Inquisition).

The Puritans were far from a united

Some religious groups, disgusted with the papistical tendencies they detected in the Church of England, sought to build a new and better society across the Atlantic, leaving friends and enemies for ever behind them.

Right: Charles I by Van Dyck. Whatever his other failings, Charles was the greatest patron of the arts of all English monarchs, largely responsible for the magnificence of the royal collection today.

group, but could be roughly divided into two classes: those, influenced by Calvinism, who wanted a radically reformed Church on the pattern of Presbyterianism in Scotland; and those who rejected the connection between Church and State, holding that the basis of the Church should be free, local congregations. The latter became known as Independents and were particularly strong in eastern England, whence Cromwell was to draw recruits for the victorious parliamentary army.

To the Presbyterians, James I was a disappointment. As James VI he had been king of Scotland since the forced abdication of his mother in 1567 (when he was a year old), but though he came from a Presbyterian country, James hated Presbyterianism and admired the English ecclesiastical settlement. Having been responsible for reintroducing bishops to Scotland, he was hardly the man to get rid of them in England.

But England presented other problems besides Puritan preachers like those James had battled with in Scotland. The most serious was money—or lack of it. The financial circumstances of the Crown were still its greatest weakness. Elizabeth, parsimonious to a fault, had been forced to sell Crown lands in her later years. James, correspondingly extravagant, was compelled to seek extra subsidies, which meant summoning parliament more often than he wished. Members of the House of Commons were growing increasingly critical of royal government, and by 1600 they had extended their criticisms into new areas. Foreign policy had always been the prerogative of the monarch, but the Commons did not care for James's policy of peace with Spain and wanted to give greater support to European Protestants in the Thirty Years' War. They argued that they had a right to criticise any policy for which they were being asked to vote taxes.

If this argument was constitutionally dubious, so was James's insistence on the "divine right" of kings to rule. James's claim that a king was answerable to none but God, though not a new doctrine in Europe, ran counter to the English tradition of consent, a tradition which, dating back to the Saxon kings, had never been entirely suppressed even in Norman times.

Like Louis XV, James I might have said *"Après moi le déluge"*. His son Charles I (1625–49), though a more kingly figure than weak-kneed, slobbering James, was also more rigid and less intelligent. After angry and unproductive confrontations with parliament, Charles resolved in 1629 to rule without it, and for eleven years he managed to do so.

Taking the country as a whole, opposition to the Crown at this stage was neither particularly dangerous nor widespread, but Charles steadily destroyed the chances of moderation by his own behaviour. He supported the

parliament to raise the money to fight the Scots. Revolt in Ireland and a general economic slump completed the destruction of government by royal decree.

Charles was in no position to resist the demands of what became known as the Long Parliament. He sacrificed both Laud and his chief minister, Strafford, to the vengeance of the House of Commons and he gave his consent to a succession of bills which were designed to make it impossible for him ever again to rule without parliament. Thus, it seemed, parliament had won the contest without fighting, for Charles had no serious support. It was not until the Puritan element in the House of Commons launched a radical attack on the ecclesiastical establishment that a conservative party began to gather around the Crown. The Grand Remonstrance, a general list of parliament's complaints and demands, was passed by only eleven votes out of 307 in the House of Com-

rigid High-Church uniformity of his unpopular archbishop, Thomas Laud, and he antagonised many people by his efforts to raise money by unusual, if not actually illegal, means. His levy of a tax to pay for shipbuilding on the whole country—it had previously been applied only to certain ports—was challenged by John Hampden, and though Hampden lost his case in the courts, immense damage was done to the reputation of royal government.

By such questionable means, Charles I was able to raise sufficient revenue to govern the country in peacetime. But not in war. When Laud's attempts to force a new prayer book on Scotland brought an enraged Presbyterian army over the border, Charles was compelled to summon

The Earl of Strafford was tried before both houses of parliament, and after the process of impeachment had failed, a bill of attainder, which did not require legal proof, was passed; the King signed the bill and saw his best minister executed in May 1641.

mons in November, 1641. Emboldened by growing support, the King forswore compromise. When the Queen, a Roman Catholic, was attacked in parliament, Charles entered the chamber with soldiers to arrest the members responsible. They had already fled, but Charles's action was outrageous and plainly illegal. Soon afterwards he left London and set up his standard at Nottingham. It was thus possible for parliament to maintain that, in law, it was the king who had rebelled, not they.

One of the oddest facts about the civil war, a period rich in paradox, is that nobody wanted it. Its outbreak was the result of the failure of that mixture of tolerance and hypocrisy (qualities sometimes more closely related than may appear) with which the English have often managed to avoid the troubles that have shaken or shattered other states.

The war was mainly a war of sieges, skirmishes and counter-marches. There were only three engagements that could be justly described as pitched battles, the first (Edgehill, 1642) ending indecisively, the others (Marston Moor, 1644, and Naseby, 1645) conclusive victories for parliament. At first, the war was fought in a curiously halfhearted spirit. Before one engagement, the parliamentary general, Waller, sent greetings to the royalist commander and assured him that the hostilities about to commence would not alter his personal affection for him. The early parliamentary leaders could not envisage a final victory: "If we beat the king ninety-nine times", said the Earl of Manchester, "yet he is still king"—an attitude that infuriated subordinate commanders like Oliver Cromwell.

Roughly speaking, the royalists held the north and west of the country, parliament the economically more prosperous south and east, including London and most of the major towns. At first parliament could not match the royalist cavalry, dashingly led by the King's son-in-law, Prince Rupert, but the navy forsook the King at the outset. What finally tipped the military scale was Cromwell's formation of the New Model Army in 1645, a formidably trained and ideologically committed professional force.

After the victory of the New Model Army at Naseby, the King was left without forces and without money to raise them. The Scots, who had entered the war on parliament's side in return for a promise to enforce Presbyterianism in England, returned home and put an end to the royalist victories of the Marquess of Montrose, who had

conducted a sensationally successful campaign on Charles's behalf in Scotland. As the war in England petered out, Charles craftily chose to surrender to the Scots, but they handed him over to parliament (for a fee).

As usual, success divided the victors

among themselves. Parliament and the army were sharply opposed: parliament wished to introduce Presbyterianism; the Puritan Independents in Cromwell's army resisted it, and a four-months arrears in their pay did not make them more amenable. In this

Below: At least one spectator fainted when King Charles I was executed in Whitehall, January 1649.
Right: A popular print of Cromwell quelling mutinous soldiers.
Far right: Cromwell reacts with horror as someone offers him the crown, though he would probably have accepted it but for the hostility of the army.

conflict, the King was both exploiter and exploited. In 1647 the army kidnapped him from parliament, thus gaining the advantage which possession of his person conferred, for neither parliament's nor the army's leaders had yet considered abolishing the monarchy. But the chances of reaching a constitutional compromise with Charles were wrecked partly by the King's duplicity, and partly by Left-wing pressure from below.

The Agreement of the People, drawn up by representatives of the lower ranks of the army, bluntly stated the doctrine of the sovereignty of the people, and demanded the vote for honest, independent citizens, regardless of property qualifications (but excluding most wage-earners). Such a programme was too radical not only

for the King or parliament, but also for Cromwell and others sympathetic to the army. At a famous meeting in Putney Church, near London, Cromwell and Ireton, his son-in-law and closest colleague, argued lengthily and courteously with the "Levellers", as they were called. The Levellers represented a minority, though a considerable one, and there were many other radical groups—like the Diggers who opposed private property altogether—whose dreams of a new social order were impracticable in the circumstances of the time. All the same, in Putney Church, the Voice of the People was heard loud and clear for the first time in English history.

Over-confident to the last, Charles rejected the moderate proposals of the army leaders and began secret nego-

tiations with the Scots, which resulted in the so-called "second civil war" in 1648. Risings in England were minor, and the Scots were resoundingly defeated by Cromwell. Charles had proved himself an impossible man to deal with, and after an embarrassingly chaotic trial, he was executed as a traitor.

Regardless of its doubtful legality, the execution of the King was a tactical mistake. Europe was shocked, and the Scots promptly recognised Charles' son (later Charles II) as king, and again invaded England. Fresh from crushing Irish rebels with bloody slaughter (the chief blot on the career of an otherwise humane statesman), Cromwell defeated the Scots at Worcester (1651). The young Charles II narrowly escaped to France.

Meanwhile, the "rump" of the Long Parliament, reduced to about sixty men after a Cromwellian purge of its members, proved incapable of dealing with the problems of government, and Cromwell, losing patience with its unproductive bickering, forcibly dissolved it altogether in 1653. But, as he recognised, the country could not be governed without king or parliament. New parliaments, equally unsatisfactory, had to be summoned, and Cromwell became king in all but name when he accepted the title of Lord Protector (1653).

The picture of Cromwell as a narrow-minded Puritan and of his rule as a mere aberration in the unruffled tradition of monarchical government is the reverse of accurate. By 17th century standards, Cromwell was broad-minded and tolerant. Even Roman Catholics were unmolested as long as they worshipped privately, and Cromwell himself enjoyed music, dancing and other un-Puritan pursuits. He was 54 when he became Lord Protector. Had he been ten years younger, the subsequent history of England would have been different. His brief rule witnessed the emergence of many of the characteristics of modern society and saw England take its place as a major international power. The universal hostility of Europe could be almost disregarded because the Cromwellian navy ruled the seas. The Netherlands, mercantile competitors, were defeated in war, Jamaica and much treasure seized from Spain, Portugal subordinated to English interests. At home, representatives from all parts of the British Isles sat in parliament for the first time, and a whole series of practical social reforms were carried out. The "New Learning" blossomed, and a multitude of talents were harnessed in the government's service. (Milton, the greatest poet of the age and staunch upholder of freedom of the press, was a Cromwellian civil servant). Cromwell was not a great art collector like Charles I, but the stories of churches desecrated by Puritan soldiers are mostly false. Cromwell protected Classical sculptures from the vandalism of the narrow-minded, he

After Cromwell's death the restoration of the monarchy was perhaps inevitable, and Charles II was welcomed at Dover by General Monck.

denounced the burning of witches, and he permitted women on the stage. Jews returned to England for the first time since their expulsion by Edward I. The law was reformed and education encouraged. There was cruelty and injustice too, but the immense moral authority of the Lord Protector was thrown into the balance on the side of moderation and tolerance in all, or nearly all, disputes.

One thing Cromwell could not provide—continuity. He had never opposed monarchy as an institution, but when offered the crown he rejected it, after much "wrestling with God" (a favourite phrase) and deterred by the likely hostility of the army. When he died in 1658 he was succeeded by his amiable and unambitious son, who lacked all authority to govern the country or command the loyalty of the army. He faded rapidly from the scene and, in the absence of other suitable candidates, Charles II (1660–85) was invited to end his French exile and take up his father's crown.

Although much of the Cromwellian legislation was repealed after the Restoration, it was impossible to put the clock back twenty years. Charles II, clever, witty and morally cynical, had no wish, as he put it, to go on his travels again, and he avoided serious conflict with parliament. Sympathetic to Roman Catholicism, he would have preferred toleration in religion, but surrendered to the general fear of "Popery", which was increasingly associated by the English with continental despotism. Charles made little effort to save those Catholics condemned in the hysterical outburst over the fictional Popish Plot, largely invented by a strange man named Titus Oates.

The dispute with the Dutch, which arose out of English efforts—en-

The naval wars with Holland in the 17th century were the result of the struggle for commercial dominance. In spite of Dutch naval superiority (in the second war at least), England's control of the Channel was the decisive factor.

shrined in the Navigation Act (1651)—to wrest the profitable carrying trade from the Netherlands, was resumed. War against Protestants was not popular—even less so when the Dutch sailed up the Medway and towed away the English flagship (1667). This shameful episode was partly excused by the confusion caused by the domestic disasters of the two previous years: the Fire of London, which destroyed three-quarters of the capital in 1665, and the last serious outbreak of plague in 1666.

An aspect of Charles's foreign policy not revealed until some years later was the chains that bound England to France in secret clauses of the Treaty of Dover (1670). Louis XIV promised a large annual payment in return for English support and Charles's promise (which he evaded) to declare himself a Catholic.

But the age of intense religious conflict was already dying, and an event as significant as the restoration of monarchy was the foundation at about the same time of the Royal Society "to promote the welfare of arts and sciences". Inspired by Francis Bacon, the Royal Society had been in embryonic existence twenty years earlier. With its formal incorporation in 1662 the age of science may be said to have begun. Among its early members were John Locke the philosopher, Christopher Wren, best-remembered for building St Paul's Cathedral, Robert Boyle, author of the fundamental law of physics concerning the expansion of gases, Robert Hooke, of whom contemporaries said there was nothing he could not do, and above all, Isaac Newton, whose basic conceptions governed the study of physics until the time of Einstein. Another member was John Evelyn, whose diary, though less fascinating (because

less personal) than that of his contemporary Samuel Pepys, gives an unsurpassed picture of the times.

The last years of Charles II's reign were dominated by attempts to exclude his brother James from succeeding to the throne. Charles managed to hand on his crown intact, but prophesied correctly that James would not be able to keep it.

James II (1685–88) was more honest but less clever than his elder brother. He made no secret of his Catholicism, and while avoiding action that was clearly unconstitutional, he pushed the rights of the Crown to extremes. When he suspended the laws against Roman Catholics, seven bish-

James II lacked his brother Charles' crafty political awareness and, as Charles had forecast, lost the throne in consequence.

ops protested. They were prosecuted for libel, but to James's chagrin the jury acquitted them. James's final mistake, paradoxically, was to produce a male heir. His daughters were both Protestants; the elder, Mary, was married to a Protestant hero, William, prince of Orange. James might have been tolerated, in spite of the hatred of his religion, until his death installed a Protestant on the throne, but the appearance of a baby prince implied a Roman Catholic dynasty. A group of leading men contacted William of Orange and invited him to invade England.

There was no resistance. James slipped away to exile in a boat that had been hopefully placed for that very purpose, and parliament declared that by leaving the kingdom he had abdicated the throne, which was therefore vacant. This convenient legal fiction allowed parliament to offer the throne to James's daughter Mary, and as she refused to reign without her husband, England acquired, for the only time in its history, joint monarchs, William III (1689–1702) and Mary II (1689–94).

The Glorious Revolution of 1688–89 was "glorious" because it was both successful and bloodless—unlike, as a later generation of Englishmen were fond of pointing out, revolutions in other countries. The constitutional settlement enshrined in the Bill of Rights, which William accepted, completed the work of the Long Parliament of 1640. It dealt mainly with specific grievances against James II, excluding Roman Catholics permanently from the throne, and it said nothing about certain constitutional questions that were to arise in the future, such as control of foreign policy. Nevertheless, it was a true revolution which buried the divine right of kings deeper than the bones of Charles I. It received its theoretical justification in the work of John Locke, who postulated a "social contract" between government and governed. A government that broke the contract might be justly removed. "Revolution", said Locke, in perhaps his most memorable statement, "is the safeguard of law".

Left: At the Battle of the Texel in 1673 the English were repulsed by the Dutch admiral, de Ruyter.

8 Trade and Empire 1689-1783

William accepted the English crown for one overriding reason: he needed England, in particular the English navy, to defend the Netherlands from Louis XIV's France. Resistance to Louis was William's life-work and he never wavered from it even in his darkest moments: persistence was his greatest virtue. But first, he had to defend his own throne. In Ireland he defeated the mixed Catholic army of James II at the battle of the Boyne (1690). The rebellion was suppressed, and the civil rights of Catholic Irish ruthlessly denied.

"King William's War", Englishmen called the war against Louis XIV, but while many blamed the King for dragging them into continental quarrels, the preservation of Holland from the French was in English interests as well as Dutch. A French invasion in support of a Stuart restoration seemed far from impossible, at least until a naval victory off Cape La Hogue (1692) denied the French command of the sea. On land, William hung on as best he could, and at the Peace of Ryswick (1697) Louis surrendered nearly all his gains of the previous twenty years. The cost of financing the war was met by the creation of the National Debt and the Bank of England, which raised large sums from investors and lent to the government at a reasonably low rate of interest.

Louis needed peace in 1697 to prepare for a greater prize. Carlos II, the last Spanish Habsburg, was dying, and preparing to leave his extensive dominions to Louis's grandson (Philippe V). Much as William disliked the prospect, the Bourbon succession in Spain would not have been opposed had not Louis, who anticipated resistance, adopted a needlessly belligerent policy. He closed French and Spanish ports to English trade and, on the death of James II, acknowledged his son as the rightful James III (the "Old Pretender"). The death of the last surviving child of Anne, heir to the English throne, had again raised the problem of the succession, and parliament responded by passing the Act of Settlement in 1701. The main purpose of the act was to prevent the return of the Stuarts and to ensure a Protestant monarchy: it therefore settled the succession on the Electress of Hanover, a granddaughter of James I, and her issue. But the act also contained constitutional provisions which, overlooked in the Bill of Rights, reflected dissatisfaction with William III. In future, the consent of parliament would be necessary for the king to make war, to leave the country, or to appoint foreigners to official positions.

As monarch William was succeeded by Anne (1702–14). As leader of the grand alliance against Louis XIV he was succeeded by John Churchill, duke of Marlborough, England's greatest general before Wellington. Marlborough's victory at Blenheim (1704) de-

Left: Queen Anne, the last reigning monarch of the Stuart dynasty, had numerous children; but none lived to survive her.
The Duke of Marlborough helped to destroy the formidable reputation of Louis XIV's armies by his victories in the War of the Spanish Succession.

stroyed the possibility of French hegemony in western Europe. From then on the French began to fall back and Marlborough's victories rolled on: Ramillies (1706), Oudenarde (1708), Malplaquet (1709). By 1709 it was clear that French expansion had been effectively checked, but equally that the Bourbon monarchy in Spain was secure. In England, the Tories demanded peace, while the Whigs were for continuing the war.

Although political parties in the modern sense hardly existed before Victorian times, the distinction between Whigs and Tories had been apparent in the reign of Charles II. Broadly, the Whigs were critical of the royal prerogative, while the Tories tended to support the Crown. Later, the Whigs became identified with the increasingly powerful commercial classes and the Tories with the traditional land-owning gentry, though both parties were usually led by great landed magnates. After the unsuccessful Jacobite (i.e. in support of James III) revolt of 1715, the Tories became tainted with Jacobitism, and that largely explained the subsequent dominance of the Whigs, which lasted until the reign of George III. However, throughout the 18th century, cliques, family connections and interest groups united members of parliament more closely than party labels.

In 1710 Queen Anne dismissed her Whig ministers, and the Tories came into power anxious to open peace negotiations. Their cause was greatly assisted by a notable political pamphlet, *The Conduct of the Allies* (1711), a devastating attack on the war by the author of *Gulliver's Travels*, Jonathan Swift, and by the accession of the Archduke Karl, the allies' candidate for the Spanish succession, to the Habsburg Austrian empire: to obtain for him a Spanish crown as well seemed distinctly superfluous. Showing scant regard for the interests of their allies, in a manner that encouraged the legend of *Albion perfide*, the English made peace at Utrecht in 1713, gaining some eastern provinces of Canada as well as Gibraltar (still held) and Minorca, and most important in the contemporary view, the right to sell slaves to the Spanish American colonies.

The Peace of Utrecht marks the arrival of Great Britain on the world stage. The name came into use after the union of the kingdoms of England and Scotland in 1707, when the Scots abolished their parliament in exchange for seats in the parliament at Westminster and the chance of sharing in England's expanding commerce. It was an act based on political common sense and mutual self-advantage and, although the immediate results were disappointing to the Scots, it vastly strengthened both countries. It is hardly possible to conceive of the British empire or the Industrial Re-

Queen Anne receives the Act of Union uniting the kingdoms of Scotland and England, which had shared the same monarch for the previous hundred years.
Below: An engagement between French and English in the Channel.

volution without the enormous Scottish contribution.

The War of the Spanish Succession had been fought chiefly in Europe, but the future contest between Britain and France, which lasted until 1815, was to be fought mainly in distant seas and far-flung lands. Fundamentally, it was a contest for trade and—as a corollary of trade—colonies. Britain was to lose one empire, but gain another, which would provide the raw materials and the markets to make the great industrial achievements of the early 19th century possible.

Although the War of the Spanish Succession marks the beginning of the

*Right: Horace Walpole, man of letters and son of the "first prime minister",
built the first and most attractive modern Gothic villa in England,
Strawberry Hill, near Twickenham.
Below: The right to vote in the 18th century was not regarded as privilege
but profit, and despite the book on political economy on the floor, this
voter no doubt expects to be handsomely for his support.*

era of imperial and maritime conflict
with France, the Treaty of Utrecht was
followed by an unusually long period
of peace. Sir Robert Walpole in England and Cardinal Fleury in France
both understood the need for re-
trenchment and endeavoured to save
their countries from the depletions of
war.

Walpole, generally acknowledged
as the first prime minister, was in most
respects a typical English country
squire; but he possessed a genius for
manipulating men and a realistic
knowledge of their weaknesses. He
came to power in the wake of the financial panic that followed the collapse of the South Sea Company in
1721. (The collapse was caused not so
much by faults of the South Sea Company itself, for in spite of its over-am-
bitious scheme to take over the National Debt it was a well-managed
organization, but by the proliferation
of more dubious enterprises which attracted hysterical "get-rich-quick" investment—a phenomenon recalling
the crazy scheme of Frobisher in
Elizabeth's reign and foreshadowing
the railway-shares bonanza of the
19th century). Walpole, who already
had a reputation for sound thinking on
finance, seemed to be the man to rescue
the country from its difficulties. He re-

Unorthodox conduct at a parliamentary polling station, as seen by William Hogarth (1697–1764), a powerfully satiric artist.

mained in power for over twenty years.

The British constitution in the 18th century was the object of almost universal commendation, earning the praise of Montesquieu and Voltaire among others. Englishmen complacently believed that they had found the way to reconcile law and liberty.

The Crown was by no means bereft of power: government was still the king's government and the king chose his ministers. But important developments in the executive had taken place in the late 17th century. Within the Privy Council (the ancient royal council) a smaller group of influential

ministers had formed, called the "cabinet council". A clause of the Act of Settlement (1701) attempted to check this development, which was regarded as undesirable, but without success. Under George I (1714–27), the inner council or cabinet frequently met without the king, who spoke no English (though he could communicate with his ministers in French). Thus a vacancy occurred which was filled by the man who could best manage his colleagues—in effect a prime minister.

What kept Walpole at the head of affairs for so long was his ability, on the one hand, to retain the confidence

of the King and, on the other, to retain sufficient support in the House of Commons. By remaining a member of the Commons, Walpole showed his awareness of the importance of the lower house and, reciprocally, contributed to its ascendancy over the House of Lords. Support in the Commons depended chiefly on patronage: the government had a great number of appointments at its disposal, and in the 18th century appointments were seldom if ever made merely on the basis of talent. The electorate was very small and a large number of parliamentary seats were exclusively controlled by landed magnates. Bribery was the rule

rather than the exception at parliamentary elections, and the chief advantage of having a vote was to sell it. Yet bribery and corruption probably had a smaller effect on events than might be supposed. If parliament had been elected more honestly and democratically, the composition of the House of Commons might not have been fundamentally different. Nearly everyone agreed that Property ruled. Few men echoed the complaints of the Levellers.

The House of Commons was no collection of yes-men. In spite of Walpole's seldom-equalled mastery of it, the House was jealous of its privileges and always ready to criticise. Indeed, some people grumbled that England had merely exchanged the tyranny of Stuart kingship for the tyranny of parliament. The fragility of even Walpole's control was illustrated by the Excise bill of 1733.

This bill was a sensible measure designed to stop the widespread evasion of customs and excise duties on wine and tobacco. If passed it would have permitted a reduction in the land tax, which landowners (who included nearly all the members of the House of Commons) were constantly demanding. Yet the bill aroused such ferocious opposition that Walpole, who always put power before principle, hastily dropped it. Its opponents had no convincing arguments against the bill on economic or social grounds, and it would have hurt no one except smugglers (admittedly, a numerous body in 18th-century England). The howls of rage which greeted the bill were chiefly an expression of resentment at Walpole's power and of a determination to make life difficult for the government.

Political conflict grew sharper in the reign of George III (1760–1820). Like Elizabeth, George III was proud of being thoroughly English. Unlike his German predecessors, he took a close interest in domestic politics and acted as the true head of the government. Whatever John Wilkes and the mob who yelled for "Wilkes and Liberty!" might say, there was nothing unconstitutional, still less tyrannical, in George's behaviour. But as the active head of the government he inevitably became a party politician, employing the vast patronage and influence at the Crown's command for partisan purposes. His greatest difficulty lay in finding a minister who was both agreeable to himself and acceptable to parliament; not until 1770 did he find what appeared to be the right man in Lord North. But unfortunately for the King, the North ministry was a disaster and lost the American colonies. (To this day, when a member of the British parliamentary opposition wishes to be really offensive to the government, he compares it with that of Lord North). It was the failure of the policy of George III and Lord North (plus the King's illness which eventually made him insane) rather than any royal usurpation of power that rang the knell of monarchical government and led to the modern system, in which ministers represent the majority party in the House of Commons and are "appointed" by the monarch merely as a matter of form.

English society in the 18th century presents a superficial appearance of social stagnation and economic progress. With political manipulators like Walpole at the head of the government, constitutional conflicts were muted, and the fear of a Jacobite revival consolidated support for the Hanoverian establishment. The threat of Jacobitism was exaggerated by the government for exactly that purpose, but the Jacobite insurrections of 1715 and 1745, while they drew little support in southern England, showed that the fears on which the Whig ministers played were not groundless.

The landed aristocracy which still formed the ruling class in England was far more intimately involved with its estates than its contemporaries in—for example—France. Landowners played a major part in the revolution in agricultural methods which was to provide the subsistence for an industrial proletariat a century hence: it was said that Walpole opened letters from his gamekeeper before official correspondence, and his closest associ-

ate in the 1720s has gone down to posterity with the nickname of "Turnip" Townshend as a result of his hearty advocacy of turnips as a field crop—a feature of the new farming methods that Townshend employed on his Norfolk estates.

The social strata were less rigid than a retrospective view suggests. Successful bankers or merchants moved easily into the landowning gentry; professional men, even tradesmen, dined at the squire's table. Younger sons, deprived of a share of the family estates by primogeniture, entered the professions or went into business.

The mass of the population were as poor as they had ever been. Some skilled craftsmen—weavers, for example—did fairly well, but the labouring masses—most still employed on the land, frequently as casual workers rather than steady wage-earners—lived in circumstances of extreme poverty. Wages varied from place to place, but the average labourer in southern England could make more money from a few hours carrying barrels for a smuggling gang than he could from a week's work on a farm. The enclosure of land, which had provoked such outcries in the 16th century, proceeded at a greater pace in the 17th and 18th, and the system of poor relief had become inadequate. In spite of individual acts of charity, rural poverty was widespread, intense, and generally ignored. Nor were conditions any better in the towns, where cheap gin turned the slums into places of real horror, graphically conveyed in the popular engravings of William Hogarth. Unfortunately, Hogarth had no literary equivalents. No age has produced fiercer satirists than Swift and Pope, but their darts were aimed at the foibles and vices of the upper class, not at the fundamental evils of society.

The Church of England, securely wedded to the political establishment, was no less complacent than lay society. Thus, when a religious revival in the second half of the 18th century produced a great religious leader in John Wesley, he was compelled, wholly against his will, to establish a new sect, Methodism, outside the Church of England. Methodism became a permanent reproach against the claim of the Church of England to be a national Church.

Rivalry in the New World brought Britain into collision with Spain, and war was declared in 1739. Walpole advised against it, but he did not resign when his advice was rejected, unthinkable behaviour for a modern prime minister. France was soon drawn into the conflict in order to prevent Britain seizing all the Spanish colonies, and the peace of 1748 was widely recognised as no more than a temporary truce. Nor was the peace everywhere observed. In India the contest continued, and Robert Clive's victories weakened the French position to the benefit of the British East India Company.

When the European war was renewed in 1756, alliances had shifted, but overseas the main antagonists were still France and Britain. A succession of brilliant successes was chiefly due to the strategic planning of William Pitt the elder, later earl of Chatham. An imperious statesman, whose proud confidence sometimes approached megalomania, Chatham seemed to exalt politics where Walpole had seemed to debase them. Besides his organizational genius, Chatham had a gift for selecting outstanding commanders, like General Wolfe, only 32 when he was mortally wounded during the daring attack on Quebec.

Wolfe's capture of Quebec ensured a British victory in North America,

William Pitt the Younger, son of the Earl of Chatham, was prime minister before the age of 24, a record never likely to be broken.

while British naval superiority secured the cream of the French West Indies and strategic outposts in West Africa and the Mediterranean. In India Clive completed his destruction of French power.

Some of these conquests were returned at the Peace of Paris in 1763, a treaty denounced by Chatham who by that time was out of office; but altogether the Seven Years' War was highly successful in terms of burgeoning British imperialism. The next round in the contest, however, was a complete disaster. This time the French were not the chief opponents, though they played a significant part in ensuring a British defeat.

By 1770 English colonists had been living in what is now the United States of America for 150 years: the thirteen colonies stretched along the east coast from Maine to Spanish Florida, and the defeat of the French in the Seven Years' War had opened new possibilities of westward expansion (though officially forbidden by a royal proclamation of 1763). The total population was about two million, about one-quarter the size of the population of England and Wales, and more than half the colonists were either of non-British descent or were native-born Americans. As it still took six weeks or more for a ship to sail from London to Boston, the colonists had become accustomed to a considerable degree of independence of the home government and, in their very different environment, had evolved a society of their own.

In the years after 1763, relations between the British government and the American colonists deteriorated rapidly. Both sides had honest grievances. The government was determined that the colonies should pay for their own defence, a costly matter in

The late 18th century was a great age for political caricature and cartoon comment, much of it now somewhat esoteric and unamusing. The conflict with the American colonists provided many opportunities for such satiric prints as that, below, of the ladies of a colonial town signing a pledge not to drink East India Company tea.

the recent war, while the colonists refused to pay British taxes without representation in the British parliament. With more justice, they resented the economic role forced upon them by prevailing mercantilist theory, which discouraged manufacturing, and the Navigation Laws, which, widely evaded hitherto, were enforced with greater rigour in the 1760s. The colonists had many sympathizers in England, including Chatham and the maverick radical Wilkes, who was involved in several important issues of civil rights in England. Most of Europe also supported the Americans, though only the French made a substantial military contribution in North America.

On the other hand, even as late as 1774, a large majority of colonists would not have supported the principles enshrined two years later in the Declaration of Independence, in spite

of the effective and dishonest propaganda of radicals like Sam Adams. It is often forgotten too that a significant minority never did accept American independence but remained loyal to Britain throughout, ultimately sacrificing their homes and livelihoods. This substantial loyalist minority was ignored by historians until recently.

The British had managed the political conflict ineptly. They managed the war no better. The surrender in 1777 of General Burgoyne and his army, stranded at Saratoga through imperfect co-ordination at the War Office, foreshadowed the final victory of Washington, although four years passed before Cornwallis surrendered at Yorktown (while a British band played "The World Turned Upside Down"), and serious fighting ended. A naval victory against the French prevented too humiliating concessions at the Treaty of Versailles in 1783.

9 Industrial Revolution and Parliamentary Reform 1780 - 1840

At the end of 1783 William Pitt the younger became prime minister at the age of 25. As a political leader, his talents were hardly less than his father's, though they lay in different areas. Upright, humane and, up to a point, liberal, Pitt laid the basis for the enlightened Conservatism of his disciples, Canning and Peel, and (though he would not have agreed) Disraeli. But Pitt had the misfortune to hold power during a period of prolonged war which delayed, damaged or destroyed his intelligent financial and economic policies. In the years before the last and longest engagement of the long Anglo-French contest, Pitt was chiefly responsible for repairing the economic damage of the earlier war and setting Britain on the path to world dominance in trade. Convinced by the arguments of the economist Adam Smith in favour of free trade (Smith's *Wealth of Nations* was published in 1776), Pitt carried through an enlightened though controversial commercial treaty with France (1786), and simplified and reduced customs and excise duties. But these policies, like his plans to reform parliament and end the slave trade, were negated by the renewal of war.

The outbreak of the revolution in France was greeted with approval in Britain. There was a certain satisfaction that France was reaping the whirlwind she had sown in America but, more amiably, a belief that the French were gaining the freedom that the English had achieved one hundred years earlier. Pitt looked forward to a long period of peaceful association. Everyone under-estimated the force of aggressive nationalism that revolution had unleashed.

By 1792 attitudes had changed drastically. Violence, massacre and war had shown that the events in France were part of something quite different from England's "Glorious Revolution". Edmund Burke had presented a powerful anti-revolutionary case in his *Reflections on the Revolution in France* (1790), a book, said the nervous George III, that everyone should read. The mob that destroyed the laboratory of Joseph Priestley, driving the great scientist to seek sanctuary in America, was motivated by hatred of Priestley's revolutionary sympathies. When the French advanced into the Low Countries, always a sensitive area for British security, war was inevitable; it was actually declared by France, February 1793, and the British reaction against the revolution was complete. Those who had ut-

BURKE
1774 — 1780

tered progressive opinions now found themselves accused of sedition. Radicals were arrested in large numbers, and political societies of a too-democratic tone were broken up. Thomas Paine, who had upheld the revolution in *The Rights of Man* (1791), was driven out of the country. The dangers of the spread of revolutionary opinions were brought home a few years later by serious mutinies in the navy at Spithead and the Nore.

The war had begun badly for Britain. The naval victory of 1 June 1794 was insufficient to offset the collapse of the anti-French European alliance, fairly despicable though that alliance was. For a time the Spanish alliance with France appeared to threaten British naval supremacy, though the victory off Cape St Vincent in 1797 restored what Englishmen regarded as the natural order of things. Meanwhile, the star of Bonaparte was rising, and Europe soon began to fold up under his driving will. His plans to strike at Britain in the east were frustrated by Nelson's victory of the Nile (Aboukir Bay) in 1798, but Marengo and Hohenlinden knocked Austria out of the war.

In 1801 Pitt temporarily resigned over George III's refusal to accept his measure for emancipating Roman Catholics, promised to the Irish in exchange for the union of the Irish with the British parliament (the Act of Union created the "United Kingdom of Great Britain and Ireland"). Pitt therefore took no part in arranging the Treaty of Amiens. It proved an abortive peace in any case; when war was renewed in 1803 Napoleon was stronger than ever, and Britain wea-

Many battles, especially naval battles, are relatively unconclusive in terms of casualties, but Trafalgar was a decided exception: twenty French or Spanish ships were taken and not one English ship lost.

ker. Pitt's fragile health was deteriorating, and the news of Napoleon's decisive victory at Austerlitz is said to have been the cause of his final collapse and death early in 1806. He was preceded to the tomb by an even greater British hero, Admiral Nelson, whose resounding victory over the combined French and Spanish fleets at Trafalgar—the most celebrated naval battle in English history—had ended any lingering danger of a French invasion in 1805.

Napoleon put more faith in indirect methods of crushing British resistance, and his continental system, which aimed to exclude British trade from Europe, inflicted severe economic hardship by denying Britain access to vital raw materials and markets. (The retaliatory British blockade of French ports, enforced by frequent interference with neutral shipping, caused a brief war with the United States in 1812). Napoleon's system was never wholly effective: the French soldiers who marched on Moscow wore British boots, and Britain's friendly relations with Portugal kept at least some European ports open.

It was largely to maintain the Portuguese contact that the future duke of Wellington waged his celebrated campaign in the Iberian peninsula, 1809–14. Although never more than a side issue, it was an increasingly enervating drain on French resources and inspired stiffer resistance to Napoleon throughout Europe. Wellington is a much underrated general (except in England) who should not be dismissed as purely a defensive commander merely because he had the valuable quality of avoiding battles that he was doubtful of winning. However, what finally destroyed Napoleon was not Wellington's success in Spain but the disastrous French invasion of Russia in 1812. Two years later it was all over. The break-out from Elba, and the 100 Days which ended at Waterloo (a near-run thing, as Wellington admitted) formed merely a brief, though resounding epilogue. At the Congress of Vienna, a conservative, in many respects reactionary, settlement of European affairs was arranged. Whatever its faults in buttressing autocratic government and denying liberal and nationalist aspirations, the settlement did at least achieve a long period of peace, a period in which the "nation of shop-keepers", as though proud of Napoleon's disparaging description, confirmed their eminence as shop-keepers to the world.

It was not only the industrial revolution that made the half century spanning the year 1800 so remarkable in English history, nor were economic institutions alone in undergoing rapid and diverse changes. This was an age of brilliant achievements and sharp conflicts. In the arts a Romantic revival was manifest in country man-

sions built as Gothic cathedrals, in the poetry of Wordsworth, Byron, Keats and Shelley, in the popular historical novels of Sir Walter Scott. But the same period witnessed the very different novels of Jane Austen, Jeremy Bentham's development of his sane if limited philosophy of utilitarianism, and Nash's elegant, Classical London terraces (Nash also designed the Brighton Pavilion, an exotic oriental palace, for the future George IV). It was an age too of out-door concerts and open-air sermons, of picnics and stage-coaches, of fox-hunting and landscape-gardening. Indeed, as the smoke of the first factories drifted across the sky, the English at last began to appreciate the beauties of their countryside, though not sufficiently to

appreciate the true worth of Constable, the painters of the Norwich school, and even the great Turner, whose greatest fame as landscape painters came to them posthumously.

The changes that turned Britain into a modern industrial state by the middle of the 19th century were neither so sudden, nor so violent, as the word "revolution" now implies, but they were certainly profound enough to deserve the term and, as economic change usually goes, they were remarkably swift. Perhaps in no other period, not even the 20th century, was

English society so thoroughly and so swiftly transformed as it was in the late 18th and early 19th centuries. This transformation did not occur out of the blue. The reason why the factory system and the associated socio-economic innovations encompassed by the term "industrial revolution" occurred in Britain earlier than in any other country was that Britain was better prepared for them.

In one sense the industrial revolution was the culmination of a series of "revolutions" going back to the mid 17th century, if not earlier. The "sci-

entific revolution" of the 17th century, though it did not lead directly to significant practical inventions, encouraged the scientific approach to nature shown by ordinary craftsmen and mechanics in their efforts to overcome immediate practical difficulties (the technological innovations of the industrial revolution were not the work of research scientists in laboratories, but of practical men in workshops). The "agricultural revolution" of the 17th–18th centuries permitted, and in some degree caused, the astonishing increase in population growth (the

population doubled between 1760 and 1830) without which rapid industrialization would not have been possible. The "transport revolution" effected by construction of canals and improvements of roads in the 18th century permitted the swift and cheap transportation of goods.

The contemporary expansion of world trade, in which Britain took the lead, provided the incentive for increased production. It was for trade that Britain's wars in the 18th century were largely fought for, since the political revolution of 1688 the commercial classes had enjoyed growing influence; one of the most powerful British institutions in the 18th century after the government itself was the East India Company—a commercial enterprise which ruled an empire. And, besides its predominant position in overseas trade, Britain possessed the largest domestic market in Europe, for France still had internal tariffs and other future rivals were not yet politically united.

All governments encouraged trade and manufacturing in the 18th century, but the British were economically more sophisticated than their neighbours. The Bank of England had been

founded as early as 1694, and Englishmen grew accustomed to dealing in bonds and notes of credit while others still looked askance at anything less solid than gold. The exact influence of this type of experience is impossible to gauge, however. At one time it was commonly said that the so-called "Protestant ethic", with its alleged virtues of thrift and hard work, played a major part in Britain's industrial progress, but that theory no longer carries much weight even among American historians.

Finally, Britain possessed the natural resources necessary to make rapid industrialization work. England had long enjoyed the advantages bestowed by numerous smooth-flowing rivers: transportation and water power. More important, Britain possessed ample supplies of coal, the fuel that, through the medium of the steam engine, provided the power for all major industry. France's coal was mostly of the wrong quality, Italy had none to speak of, Germany's was undiscovered, Belgium's unexploited; but England, Scotland and Wales each possessed large and accessible deposits. It was around the coalfields that the new industrial cities grew, especially in the

A statue of the Scottish scientist James Watt (1736–1819) in Birmingham.

There were steam engines of a sort before Watt, but he invented the condensing *steam engine*, a vastly superior notion, as well as many less fundamental improvements.

English Midlands and north, thus creating a cultural division between north and south that visitors still notice.

The pattern of development in different industries was often similar, though occurring at different times. First came a period of accelerating production by traditional methods. When those methods were fully stretched, and demand was still rising, some kind of technical breakthrough was made, permitting much higher productivity and in turn encouraging more innovations to make connected processes comparably efficient. The classic example is the textile industry, more specifically the manufacture of cotton, which was the first industry to undergo the process of transformation from domestic craft to mechanized mass-production, and led the way in Britain's booming export trade.

In the early 18th century cotton manufacture was increasing rapidly, with more and more individual spinners and weavers employed. The invention of the flying shuttle (1733) made weaving a faster process, so that one weaver could keep five or six spinners busy. That created pressure for a speed-up of spinning, effected first by Hargreaves's spinning mule (1773), which increased productivity several hundred times. Weaving thus lagged behind—until Cartwright's power loom (1775) brought it into line. Of course, new inventions were not perfected until some time after their first invention, nor were they immediately introduced everywhere as soon as they were perfected. There were more hand looms than power looms as late as 1830. Nevertheless, the revolution in the cotton industry was virtually complete in less than fifty years, and by 1820 the phenomenon of the industrial city, with all its unanticipated

problems, had appeared in Lancashire.

The manufacture of iron and steel underwent a similar pattern of development, but other industries, like coal-mining, depended not so much on technological improvements (though more efficient steam-driven pumps allowed deeper mining) as on a simple concentration of labour.

The factory system created a new society in Britain. At the top was a new class of massively rich industrialists and entrepreneurs, often men from a poor economic background. They included many whom it is hard to admire and some who were plain crooks, but also heroic figures such as Josiah Wedgwood (pottery) and Matthew Boulton (metals), men of liberal principles and strong intellectual interests

who founded "Literary and Philosophical" societies in cities like Manchester, Birmingham and Liverpool. Such men were a weighty influence in society, their great economic power bringing political power in its wake. Sir Robert Peel the elder, one of the richest manufacturers in the country, was the son of a poor farmer and the father of a prime minister.

The industrial proletariat was formed from surplus agricultural labourers and redundant craftsmen. The workers had no economic and no political power. Their general living conditions, long hours and low pay, were deplorable, though it is not certain that, by and large, they were any worse than before. What made their situation uniquely grim was their sheer numbers and concentration in cities:

rural poverty seems less horrible because more scattered. The prevailing doctrine of *laissez-faire*, which explained Britain's economic success as the result of non-interference by government, prevented action to alleviate the conditions of the working class, though there were a few enlightened employers who grasped the fact that better pay and conditions would lead to more profit, not less. The idealistic proto-socialist, Robert Owen, proclaimed, not without effect, the doctrine that the way to national prosperity was through co-operation, not competition.

In fact, while real wages remained very low, for most people and for most of the time during the 19th century wages were rising slightly faster than prices. Periodic slumps brought hardship to a great number, and without doubt there was a large minority, often overlooked in statistics, who lived close to destitution. According Charles Booth, 30 per cent of the Londoners were in that category as late as 1888.

Organization of labour was slight, inneffective and, more to the point, illegal—at least until the laws against trade unions were partly relaxed in 1825. Early unions gained a few concessions but tended to pursue grandiose ideals of little concern to the masses. The first Trades Union Congress was not held until 1868 and it was only in the 1880s that socialism was seriously revived, this time in a more practical and mundane form.

The painful slowness of social improvement makes a striking contrast with the rapidity of industrial progress. When the government did begin to accept a measure of responsibility for industrial conditions, for example in a series of Factory Acts which limited the hours of work for children, the legislation was widely ignored because no authority existed to enforce it. The industrial revolution was a thoroughly haphazard affair; the idea of planning was foreign to it, and the gravest problems of early industrial society arose from the total absence of a civil bur-

eaucracy, of factory inspectors, housing officers, health officers, even regular police. Welfare depended entirely on charity, and although charity was a not uncommon virtue in the 19th century, it could have little effect on the fundamental problems of society.

Those problems could be approached only along the path of political reform.

The issues in which John Wilkes had been involved in the 1760s and 1770s had protected the rights of voters, stopped the government making arrests on unspecified charges, and ensured freedom to report debates in parliament; while in 1772 slavery had been declared illegal in England (though it was not abolished in the British empire until 1833). But these were victories for the common law; the institutions of government remained unchanged, in some cases since the Middle Ages. Members of parliament were still elected on the system that had existed in Elizabethan times, with the result that a sparsely populated

*Left: For centuries,
the main fish market in London
was at Billingsgate.*

*Below: These comparatively civilized conditions in the Middlesex Hospital
were not typical of 18th-century medical care*
*Bottom: Bankers and brokers, observed by the prolific watercolourist and
draughtsman, Thomas Rowlandson, late 18th century.*

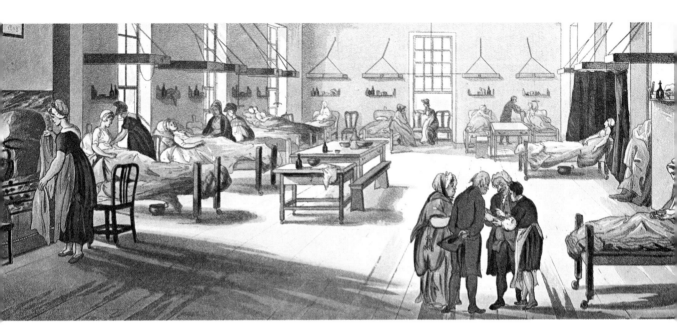

county like Cornwall had 44 members of the House of Commons while great and growing cities like Manchester and Birmingham had none at all. Voting qualifications had hardly changed in 400 years, resulting in enormous discrepancies and numerous individual absurdities: a few constituencies had less than ten voters each. Reform of parliament, however unattractive to the great patrons who controlled large numbers of seats, was widely seen to be necessary; the Whigs supported it and the *Times,* already established as a powerful organ of opinion, constantly advocated it.

Since the time of the younger Pitt, government had been dominated by the Tories, who included reactionaries like Wellington as well as liberals like George Canning, Pitt's ablest disciple. However, not even Canning regarded parliamentary reform as a prime objective; he classed democracy with despotism as "the two bigotries", and acquired his liberal reputation through his foreign policy, especially his espousal of the new states emerging in

South America. Canning died in 1828 and two years later, amid rising demands for reform, Wellington became prime minister. His reactionary stance caused a break with the Canningite wing of the party, while his acceptance of a bill admitting Roman Catholics to parliament alienated the Right wing. As frequently happened in any critical situation in the 19th century, politics were plunged into confusion and party labels became an unreliable guide.

The confusion at Westminster reflected the situation in the country. It was an unsettled time, with outbreaks of machine-breaking and agrarian riots. The death of George IV (1820–30) made a general election necessary, at which many supporters of reform were elected, and the Tories retired for a long sojourn in the wilderness. Reform now seemed inevitable; nevertheless, there ensued two years of intense excitement, including another general election, two resignations by the prime minister, Earl Grey, and heavy though reluctant pressure by King William IV (1830–37) on the

House of Lords, before the Great Reform Bill was passed.

The Reform Act of 1832 represented a victory for the middle class. It redistributed parliamentary seats more equably and introduced a new voting qualification, the effect of which was to give the vote to the urban middle class, plus some others like tenant farmers and a few skilled craftsmen. After all the fuss, its practical results were small. The composition of the House of Commons after the act was little different than before, and the great mass of the population was still excluded from politics. Yet the act was highly significant, representing a break in the ramparts of property and privilege which has been widening, in fits and starts, ever since. Its opponents objected that the act would be bound to lead to more radical reform in future, and they were right. However, the act was swiftly accepted by almost everyone, and it was followed in 1835 by a parallel reform of local government, which introduced local elected councils.

Disappointment with the results of the Reform Act and dislike of the well-meant but inhumane Poor Law Act of 1834 were partly responsible for the movement known as Chartism. The Charter which gave it its name was drawn up in 1838; it demanded universal male suffrage and other reforms that seem very moderate now but were regarded as dangerous then. The movement attracted considerable working-class support and its leaders included some admirable and enlightened men as well as a few rascals. What worried the ruling class was that Chartism appeared to be a cover for revolutionary opinions and social protests of all kinds. There were riots in many parts of the country in 1839, and Chartism enjoyed a revival in 1848, the "year of revolution". But Britain in that famous year was alone among major European states in avoiding violent revolution. On several occasions in the previous thirty years revolution had seemed possible, even likely. But after 1848 violence receded. Some Chartist objectives were fulfilled by subsequent acts of parliamentary reform in 1867 and 1884; other social reforms, plus a rising standard of living, made Britain in the second half of the 19th century a more stable society than it had appeared in the first half, encouraging greater national confidence.

Opposite above: The scene in Covent Garden market during election time.
Below: George IV, the "first gentleman of Europe" in coronation robes. He was responsible for much expenditure for which, however, frivolous at the time, we may now be grateful, for otherwise Brighton Pavilion, for example, would not exist.

10 Victorian Britain 1840-1900

"Commerce", said Richard Cobden (1804–65), "is the grand panacea, which, like a beneficent medical discovery, will serve to inoculate with the healthy and saving taste for civilization all the nations of the world." His belief in the beneficial consequences of trade was shared by many people in 19th-century Britain.

Cobden was one of the leaders of the "free-trade" movement, which demanded a clean sweep of the antiquated duties and restrictions on trade comparable with the parallel demand for political reform. Pitt had moved some way towards free trade, but the onset of war had aborted his policy. After 1815 the momentum was re-newed by Pitt's disciples, notably William Huskisson, the accident-prone president of the Board of Trade (he was run over by the locomotive at the opening ceremony of the Liverpool and Manchester Railway in 1830). However, progress towards free trade was nothing like fast enough to satisfy men like Cobden and the manufacturers of Manchester. The argument raged most fiercely over the Corn Laws.

The purpose of the Corn Laws was to protect the agricultural interest—landowners chiefly, but also tenant farmers and labourers dependent on low rents—by duties levied on imported grain. The industrial and com-mercial interest opposed them because they kept the price of bread high. The situation was rather more complicated than that, and in fact the worst fault of the Corn Laws was that for various reasons they failed in their primary purpose of keeping the price of bread relatively stable. Sir Robert Peel, who began his notably productive ministry in 1841, was sympathetic to the arguments of the Anti-Corn Law League (founded in Manchester in 1839), which, through the medium of railways and the penny post (introduced 1840) disseminated its propaganda with speed and vigour. But while he introduced a series of measures reducing customs and excise duties on other

Opposite page: From the Great Reform Act of 1832, the House of Commons progressed rapidly to the height of its power and glory during the Victorian era.
Right: The House of Lords in the early 19th century.

goods, replacing the lost revenue with an income tax (which he incorrectly forecast as a temporary expedient only), Peel left the Corn Laws inviolate until 1845. In that year, general scarcity—the decade was called the Hungry Forties—was aggravated by failure of the potato crop, a major disaster for Ireland where it was the staple food. The resulting famine made up Peel's mind, and in the teeth of ferocious opposition from two-thirds of his own party, he forced the repeal of the Corn Laws through parliament. His action split his party, which did not regain a safe majority in the House of Commons until 1875, and ended his political career (he died soon afterwards).

Like so many great causes fought long and hard to a successful conclusion, the repeal of the Corn Laws had little immediate political effect. Bread prices hardly fell, and the Irish famine was not checked. Farmers were not ruined as some had gloomily forecast: the agricultural depression in England set in thirty years later. But besides destroying the old Tory party (the name Conservative, disliked by Benjamin Disraeli who had led Tory opposition to Peel, was already coming into use), the long dispute between "Protection" and "Free Trade", hardened antagonism between the landowning and the commercial-manufacturing interests. Its result was a resounding victory for the latter and was also the decisive victory of free trade. The Navigation Laws, enacted in the 17th century to protect English trade and English shipping, were repealed in 1849; such was the dominance of the Royal Navy and British commerce that they were evidently unnecessary. Disraeli never revived the policy of protection, fiercely though he had defended it against Peel.

The victory of free trade was followed by a period of great and growing prosperity for Britain: in the generation after 1850, the value of foreign trade rose about 400 per cent.

The spirit of liberalism which had brought about the Reform Act of 1832 and the Repeal of the Corn Laws in 1846 was also at work in the British empire. Slavery was abolished in 1833 (with large compensatory payments to West Indian planters) and soon afterwards the first step was taken towards turning the empire into the "Commonwealth". Cobden had asserted that giving freedom to the colonies would result in economic advantage to the mother country because it would create greater freedom of trade. Britain's valuable connections with the United States, which provided most of the raw material for the Lancashire cotton industry, could be said to support that view.

A rebellion in French-populated Quebec, suppressed without great difficulty, was the cause of Lord Durham's investigation which culminated in his famous Report on Canada (1839), the foundation document of liberal imperialism. The report advocated a political system that was appreciably more democratic than the current British system, with a large degree of self-government—seen by Lord Durham as the only means of creating a sense of national unity. The report stopped well short of full self-government, reserving foreign policy and certain other matters to the British government, but during the period between the Durham report and the British North America Act (1867), most of the reservations disappeared. The act of 1867 formed the constitutional basis for a united confederation, essentially autonomous.

A similar approach was taken to the development of Australia and New Zealand, where the problems were more easily solved partly because the settlers were predominantly British. But the Cape Colony of South Africa had, like Quebec, a majority of non-British—in this case, Dutch—colonists. Restless under British control, many Boers ("farmers"), set out north-eastward on the Great Trek,

97

The young Queen Victoria made a pleasant change as monarch after a succession of fat and elderly gentlemen.

founding new republics on the Orange River and in Natal. British expansion led to the take-over of Natal, while the Orange Free State remained, for the time being, independent. But the conflicting interests of Boers, British and Bantu promised future troubles.

Meanwhile, the British people enjoyed unparallelled peace and prosperity—or, at least, the middle classes did. After the disturbances of the earlier part of the century, security seemed assured. British institutions had demonstrated their ability to bend and change with the shifting winds of industrialization, reform, and imperial expansion. The Whig historian Macaulay pointed to the continuity of British history, a comforting stability symbolized, at the peak of society, by the monarchy.

Reigning longer than any other English monarch, Queen Victoria (1837–1901) rescued the Crown from the disrepute into which it had fallen during the reigns of her uncles, the frivolous George IV (1820–30) and the mundane William IV (1830–37). It is unlikely that she would have made much impression on history if she had not inherited the Crown and worn it so long; but her ordinariness was of an inspired kind. She instinctively identified with the beliefs and aspirations of her subjects, specifically her middle-class subjects (she was not much impressed by the aristocracy, and towards the working class she was sympathetic but, inevitably, ignorant). One of her prime ministers said that when he knew Her Majesty's thoughts on any subject, he had a good idea of what the middle classes thought too. Until 1861, the Queen was greatly assisted by her German husband, Prince Albert, who typefied many of the virtues of the mid-Victorian gentleman and, in the opinion of Disraeli, did

Three Victorian politicians. Top: Lord Palmerston, the chief influence in foreign policy for many years until his death in 1865. Centre: Benjamin Disraeli, later Lord Beaconsfield, witty Jewish novelist who directed and inspired a greater British Empire. Bottom: William Gladstone, the "Grand Old Man" of the Liberal party, morally the most impressive British statesman of modern times.

more for England than any of her native kings. Disraeli also made the characteristically provocative remark that if Albert had lived longer, he might have given the country "the blessings of absolute government"; but in fact the monarchy in the second half of the 19th century had virtually no direct power. By sheer hard work and determination, Albert made it a force to be reckoned with, but after his death Victoria retired into masochistic widowhood and resented even routine government business. Nevertheless, her private influence was far from negligible. In her later years the formidable little old woman in a plain linen bonnet, having long forgotten Albert's liberalism, fiercely supported the Conservative party and sometimes made the life of her devoted but (by her) detested Liberal prime minister, Gladstone, a thorough misery.

The British in the mid-Victorian era had some reason to feel complacent. Unfortunately, complacency often declined into an unattractively smug self-satisfaction and, in time, subsided into mere stagnation. The signs of that were not yet apparent, however, and it would be wrong to dismiss mid-Victorian society as too selfadmiring and materialist. It produced plenty of critics: the poet and educationist Matthew Arnold assaulted philistinism in *Culture and Anarchy* (1869); the puritanical moralist Thomas Carlyle fiercely goaded his contemporaries and asserted the moral superiority of medieval society in *Past and Present* (1845); the novelist Charles Dickens satirized official incompetence and fraud and poignantly portrayed the misery of poverty in a succession of marvellously inventive novels. The mere fact that so much is known about social distress in Victorian England is a tribute of a kind to Victorian con-

sciences. Certainly, many of the solutions proposed seem to us thoroughly inadequate, and the sneer that humane critics of society like Dickens were closer to Santa Claus than Karl Marx is unkind but not inaccurate.

Any generalization about the Victorians, especially in the realm of ideas, is liable to mislead, because it was an age of variety and eclecticism (all too apparent, sometimes, in its architecture). For example, in the year—1859—that Samuel Smiles published his best-seller, *Self-Help*, extolling the virtues of individualism, competition and the get-ahead spirit, John Stuart Mill published his great essay *On Liberty* and Charles Darwin, with some trepidation, produced his shattering work *On the Origin of Species*. Meanwhile, in the reading room of the British Museum, Karl Marx was making notes for *Das Kapital* (1867).

The Victorians believed in the improvement, if not perfectability, of human society, if not human nature, through the means of material progress which marched hand-in-hand with moral improvement. Hence the intense, almost religious excitement attending the Great Exhibition of 1851, an extraordinary display of British superiority in manufacturing and technical innovation which was housed in a vast palace of glass so high it enclosed full-sized elm trees growing on the site. The leading organizer of this great show was the tireless Prince Albert who, in a speech at the time, described the exhibition as "a living picture of the point of development at which the whole of mankind has arrived . . . and a new starting point from which all nations will be able to direct their further exertions". The Prince Consort looked forward to "that great end, to which, indeed, all

Some drawbacks of democracy, as seen in this French impression of elections in England, published 1841.

In 1844 Queen Victoria and Prince Albert made a courtesy visit to the French fleet.

affairs, his domestic policy was generally conservative. Taxation remained low and social reforms were few and limited; the Second Reform Act (1867) could not be passed until Palmerston had passed from the scene. Sweeping changes were not effected until the first ministry (1868–74) of W. E. Gladstone and the early years of the Disraeli ministry (1874–80). Gladstone began his unparallelled career as a stern, unbending Tory and ended it well to the left of the Liberal party that was largely his creation. His first and greatest ministry established the modern civil service, with entry based on talent instead of influence, and carried out a major reform of the legal system and the courts. As far as the general welfare of the population was concerned, perhaps the greatest advances were those made in education and public health—the latter hastened by devastating outbreaks of cholera.

Palmerston's foreign policy was broadly based on the necessity of maintaining the balance of power in Europe. Thanks to Britain's commercial and naval strength, he was able to assert British interests in a forthright and chauvinistic manner, which modern British governments occasionally look back to with ill-disguised envy. The famous Don Pacifico incident illustrated Palmerston at his most "Palmerstonian". In origin a Spanish Jew, Don Pacifico was a naturalized Portuguese living in Athens who claimed British citizenship through having been born in Gibraltar. During antisemitic rioting, his house was burned, and he lodged a claim for damages against the Greek government. Two years later, the fleet being in the eastern Mediterranean, Palmerston ordered a blockade of the Greek coast until Don Pacifico was paid. De-

history points—*the realization of the unity of mankind*". This was to be accomplished, apparently quite soon, by "*the great principle of division of labour*, which may be called the moving power of civilization". Besides the boggling astonishment we may feel at the extraordinary confidence of the Victorians in their own achievements and prospects, perhaps there is also a twinge of envy.

Prince Albert also referred to the part to be played by Almighty God in achieving the great end that he predicted. Though not a very religious man himself, he could hardly have avoided doing so, for this was the last great age of religious faith. The established Church of England, which two or three generations earlier had begun to look almost moribund, was both shaken and stimulated by conflicting factions: on the left, mission-conscious Evangelicalism, often allied in moral concerns with nonconformist sects; on the right, the ritualistic High Anglicanism of the Oxford movement which, notably in the case of John Henry Newman, sometimes carried its adherents over the brink into Roman Catholicism; occupying the middle ground the Broad Church movement, hardly a "movement" in itself but embracing a wide spectrum of theological opinion. But, even in England, only about half the church-going population were members of the Church of England. Roman Catholics formed a small minority (in Ireland a large majority). Others belonged to the Methodist, Baptist and other "dissenting" Protestant Churches.

For twenty years after the fall of Peel, politics were dominated by the genial figure of Lord Palmerston. In contrast with his initiatives in foreign

fending himself against criticism of this high-handed action, Palmerston made a famous speech in which he spoke of a *pax Britannica*, which had replaced the *pax Romana* of ancient times, and asserted that wherever a British subject might be, he would be guarded against injustice by the watchful eye and strong arm of England. Such ideas went down very well with an increasingly chauvinistic public.

But Palmerston, again reflecting the feelings of the mass of people, was sympathetic to the forces of liberalism and nationalism in Europe—so long as they did not conflict with British interests. Tacit British support for Garibaldi in Italy infuriated the established powers of Europe. Indeed, Palmerston's popularity with the British people was balanced by the loathing he arroused in the conservative courts of Europe.

A major consideration affecting British foreign policy in the 19th century was the weakness of the Turkish empire and the fear of Russian expansion: the "Eastern Question". It was the reason for Britain's involvement in the Crimean War (1854–56). The war solved nothing, but had some useful indirect results in the reform of the army under Gladstone's government and the revolution in nursing resulting from the work of Florence Nightingale, "the lady with the lamp". Apart from the Crimean war, Britain kept out of European wars in the 19th century. Palmerstonian bluster did not prevent the Austro-Prussian seizure of Schleswig-Holstein; still less did Britain interfere with Bismarck's forging of the *Reich*. The outbreak of the civil war in America created tension, but Palmerston wisely resisted the desire of

some of his colleages to recognise the South as a sovereign power. As it was, the raids of the *Alabama*, a Confederate cruiser built in Britain, infuriated the Union, and in 1872 Gladstone's government paid a large indemnity for the losses inflicted by the *Alabama* on Yankee merchant ships.

The "Eastern Question" came to a head again in the 1870s, and the ageing Disraeli roused himself sufficiently to make a considerable effect at the Congress of Berlin (1878). He returned to England with Cyprus in his pocket and the claim that he had brought back "Peace with Honour", though to the duke of Argyll, an old ally of Gladstone, it sounded more like "Retreat with Boasting".

Looking back, it is easy to see that Britain reached its peak in the mid Victorian period and that a decline set in about 1875 that has never been re-

Daniel O'Connell, Irish leader, expert organiser of mass appeals, was largely responsible for the act which lifted civil disabilities from Roman Catholics in 1829.

Charles Parnell's oratory and organization acquired more power for Irish members of the Commons than their numbers seemed to warrant. Parnell finally compelled Gladstone to embrace the cause of Home Rule for Ireland.

versed. Naturally, contemporaries did not realise that the troubles of the 1870s were more than a temporary setback: in some respects Britain appeared more powerful, not less, thirty years later, as a result of the expansion of the British empire by nearly 10,000,000 square kilometres during the last two decades of the 19th century.

The economic slump of the 1870s was not confined to Britain, but its results were more significant there than anywhere else. When a succession of bad harvests counided with sharp American competition in grain, agriculture fell into a decline that was to last until the Second World War. In the 1860s the British, in a good year, were almost capable of feeding themselves; a generation later they had to import 70 per cent of their food.

The ongoing industrial revolution had faltered before, in the 1840s, but then it had been pulled out of its slump by the railways boom and the British adoption of free trade. This time there was no comparable development. To protect their farmers against cheap American wheat, continental governments began erecting tariff barriers. The Americans retaliated, which provoked further reactions in Europe. Within a few years, free trade had been abandoned. But Britain, conservative as always and loth to abandon the system on which its prosperity had been built, clung to the old principle and suffered accordingly.

A failure to change with the times was already affecting industry. The Paris Exhibition of 1867 had revealed that British technology was no longer so far advanced as it had appeared in

the London exhibition of 1851. The organization and growth of industry was held in check by what an American writer called "the dead hand of past achievement". Small family firms were run by untalented grandsons, with old techniques and low investment; there was no state support and little technical education. By the 1880s Britain was no longer the leading industrial power. Germany and the United States were drawing ahead, while France and other countries were moving up fast.

Marked changes were evident in society, arising partly out of the deterioration in Britain's economic position. Social and political conflicts grew sharper; the divisions in society yawned more widely. The early 1870s were a period of increased industrial unrest, and the slump brought unemployment and disillusionment. Strikes were more frequent and more bitter. The working class turned away from the old alliance with Liberalism, and the first Labour members appeared in the House of Commons. But in politics the most divisive factor was the Irish Question.

The English had already had some seven centuries in which to find an answer to the Irish Question, but they had failed (someone once complained, not wholly without justice, that whenever the English found an answer, the Irish changed the question). The most recent attempts to solve the problem constitutionally, the Act of Union (1800) and the Roman Catholic Emancipation Act (1829) had not only failed to attract Irish approval, they had created a position in which Charles Parnell's tight-knit group of Irish members held the political balance in the House of Commons. Gladstone's ameliorative legislation—revoking the privileged position of the Irish (Protestant) Church, tackling the crucial question of land ownership—did not appease the nationalists, who demanded Home Rule.

In 1882 Gladstone was converted to Home Rule and he came into office four years later with that commitment. On this issue the Liberal party split like an apple. Anti-Home Rule Liberals joined the Conservatives as the "Unionist" party (the name survives for the party in Northern Ireland) but when someone asked Gladstone, in astonishment, whether he meant to go on with Home Rule in face of the defection of his senior colleagues, the "Grand Old Man" characteristically replied that he would go on without anybody. The Home Rule bill was defeated in the Commons, Gladstone called a general election (1886), and lost. Seven years later he was back in power, now aged 82. With the aid of a motley coalition he forced his bill through the House of Commons

largely by the force of his indomitable will, but in the House of Lords it was rejected by a large majority. The vote effectively ended Home Rule. In Ireland, the more militant Sinn Fein ("Ourselves") movement arose, demanding complete independence from Britain.

Another aspect of change in British society in the last quarter of the 19th century was a new attitude towards colonies: the "new imperialism". Britain was not the only country to indulge in a massive colonial land-grab; the fever for colonies affected every nation with the capacity to gratify it; but Britain took the lead and acquired the most territory.

The "new imperialism" represented a startling departure in British colonial policy. It has been said that Britain acquired its empire in a fit of absence of mind, and there is a grain of truth in the remark. Certainly, successive British governments had regarded colonial

entanglements with strong misgivings and had generally tried to avoid them. Missionaries or merchants who advocated British settlements in Africa were invariably snubbed. Disraeli remarked in the 1850s that colonies were "a millstone round our necks", though he changed his mind later. At that time, the attitude to Britain's colonial possessions was one of trusteeship. The ideas embodied in Lord Durham's report on Canada were current; it was generally assumed that the British dominions would become independent in time, perhaps quite a short time. There was no talk of an empire on which the sun never—never would—set. Britain had a responsibility to less fortunate peoples, to give them the benefits of Christianity, economic development, individual freedom (policy towards the colonies was often more liberal than policy at home). Such ideas may have been naive, even disastrously inappropriate in many respects, but they

One of the by-products of empire was the appearance of a rich and exotic gallery of gorgeous princes, like those who assembled for this ceremony in Delhi in 1861.

were not insincere nor ignoble. David Livingstone did not march across Africa for the benefit of British imperialism; his predominant, if foggy, motive was "to do something for Africa".

By the 1880s, attitudes had changed. In a famous course of lectures on *The Expansion of England*, Professor J. R. Seeley expressed the belief that "there is something fantastic in all those notions of abandoning the colonies or abandoning India". Empire had become Britain's "manifest destiny". A note of coarseness and vul-

garity sounded through the drum-banging pronouncements of British greatness. Imperialists like Cecil Rhodes and the German-born Alfred Milner betrayed a streak of overt racism in their assertions of British superiority. Imperialism was popular with the masses, and as the franchise became more democratic, the Conservative party found it a tempting vote-catcher. But Liberal governments could not or would not reverse the trend. It was Gladstone, who heartily loathed every manifestation of the new

imperialism and described it as "an odious system of bluster and swagger, and of might against right", who gave the order for the fleet to bombard Alexandria in 1882.

Gladstone described one of the nastier and newer aspects of imperialism. On the whole, British colonies were remarkably well governed, better than those of any other colonizing power. It is easy to forget that British rule always depended to some extent on the consent of the ruled. The Indian Mutiny (1857) was not a nationalist re-

In old age Queen Victoria became a symbol as powerful and, it seemed, as permanent as the British Empire itself.

volt against alien rule but essentially a conservative reaction against the introduction of modern educational and economic methods. The British nowhere had the men to rule by force. Though they were involved in many colonial wars—some, like the "opium wars" in China, dishonourable—they were ill-equipped to deal with a serious nationalist revolt, as the victories of the South African Boers showed in 1899. Nor were the old ideas of service and trusteeship dead beneath the tawdry glitter of the new imperialism. The

general standard of colonial officials was high. The concept of "the white man's burden", which now seems absurd if not worse, was not totally hypocritical.

The scramble for colonies in Africa came to a head simultaneously in north and south. At Fashoda on the upper Nile, a French force expanding from the west was confronted by Kitchener's army moving south. Britain and France teetered on the brink of war, until the French withdrew. In the south, the long conflict between the

British and the Boers broke into open war. The Boers had many supporters in Britain and almost universal support in Europe.

The war was a salutory experience: it revealed the fragility of British power when challenged and the general unpopularity of Britain among its European neighbours. In those sabre-rattling days, when the peoples of Europe seemed to be contemplating war as some kind of uplifting—and anyway inevitable—experience, the British began to look about for allies. They found them eventually in France and Russia—an unlikely team in view of Britain's history. The plans were being drawn up for Armageddon.

11 War and Waning Powers 1900-1945

"The lamps are going out all over Europe", said Lord Grey, British foreign minister, on the night that the First World War began. "We shall not see them lit again in our lifetime". Later generations concurred in this grim prophesy.

It has often been said that the First World War was a dreadful mistake, the result of a complex mixture of conflicting ambitions, new social forces, irresponsible leadership and real misunderstandings; but in view of what is now known of German policies it is difficult to see how the "mistake" could have been avoided. For Britain, however, it was a mistake in more ways than one. Besides embarking on a national effort never justified by the issues at stake, Britain adopted a disastrous revolution in foreign policy: a reinvolvement on a massive scale in European power struggles, which the British had generally avoided since the 15th century. It is still not wholly clear how Britain became involved. Besides the agreements with France and Russia, in themselves a thorough reversal of traditional British attitudes, there was much secret diplomacy, involving the individual ambitions of powerful men. Certainly the war was no popular crusade, although propaganda (which did not shrink from fictional atrocity stories of butchered Belgian babies) soon made it so, and the outbreak of hostilities was greeted with extraordinary displays of popular enthusiasm based on ignorance of what modern war involved.

In the 1920s people blamed the troubles of their time on the war and its immediate consequences; but in reality many of those troubles were already emerging before 1914.

The population of Britain in 1914 was about 43 millions and still increasing, though at a slower rate (the rate has, with peaks and troughs, continued to decline and is now almost stationary). Trade was still expanding, and the total value of Britain's trade in 1913 exceeded that of Germany; but it was concentrating more and more on the economically underdeveloped countries of the empire, because competition had reduced Britain's share of other markets. The British navy was still the largest in the world, in spite of German efforts to overtake it, but it no longer fulfilled the old ideal of matching any two foreign fleets. Agriculture had made a partial recovery from the slump of the 1870s, but Britain still imported more than three-quarters of the grain it consumed. Altogether, the economy remained superficially strong, but its deficiencies were serious and were to be clearly revealed by the pressures of war. Vulnerable (and distant) markets and sources of raw materials, old-fashioned methods of production, dependence on traditional industries like chemicals and electrical engineering, disproportionate reliance on "invisible" industries like banking and insurance: these weaknesses were to be revealed, though not corrected, by war.

The distribution of Britain's considerable wealth remained highly inequitable. About two per cent of the population owned over 80 per cent of the national wealth, although some efforts had been made to readjust the balance—for instance, by increased death duties. The role of the state, which was to be massively expanded by war, was already increasing, and the government was adopting a larger responsibility for social welfare. Compulsory unemployment insurance and limited old-age pensions were introduced by the "Welsh wizard", David Lloyd George, the outstanding political talent of the first quarter of the 20th century. Education still lagged behind the progress made in Germany or France, but several new universities were opened and the school-leaving age was raised. Traditional institutions of education were still dominated by the classics, but science was making large strides. In his laboratory at Cambridge, Ernest Rutherford was laying the basis for nuclear physics.

Political change was confined within the bounds of peaceful reform, though there was industrial unrest and a series of strikes in 1911, caused by rising prices and the influence of French syndicalism. The infant Labour party,

106

Edward VII, acknowledging a cheering crowd in Paris, played a small part at least in promoting the Entente Cordiale.
Bottom: There were outbreaks of violence and strikes before the Great War but, as this photograph shows, both rioters and police might have learned much from their successors in the 1970s.

soon to replace the Liberals as the main party of the Left, had substantial representation in parliament. The forces of reaction were defeated by the Parliament Act, which ended permanently the ability of the hereditary House of Lords to reject financial legislation or to impose more than a brief delay on any other bill passed by the elected House of Commons. Democracy seemed to be working better than expected, though the stubborn refusal to extend the vote to women encouraged militant tactics by the Suffragettes. The war, rather than the stone-throwing of Mrs Pankhurst and her comrades, eventually secured the vote, though women under thirty were barred until 1928.

Besides British women, the Irish were excluded from the exercise of true democracy. Home Rule was accepted by the Liberal government and only the outbreak of war in 1914 postponed its enactment. But the Easter Rising in Dublin in 1916, by arousing widespread sympathy for Sinn Fein in Ireland, made the limited self-government of Home Rule finally redundant. The Rising was suppressed by British troops; civil war broke out in 1920 and a settlement, unsatisfactory though it has since proved, divided the country into the Irish Free State (independent but with some restrictions) and the province of Northern Ireland, where the Protestant majority successfully insisted on their right to remain a part of the United Kingdom.

Britain declared war in August 1914 when Germany attacked neutral Belgium. In Europe the hostilities soon fell into a pattern from which no general on either side could break out—a war of attrition, in which defence was comparatively simple and attack immensely difficult and costly. Compulsory military service was in-

The Royal Navy was still formidable in 1914, though its traditional policy of maintaining parity with the next two largest fleets in the world had been abandoned in face of Germany's mighty new fleet.

troduced in Britain for the first time early in 1916, when many regular regiments had been decimated by artillery, machine guns and barbed wire amid the engulfing Flanders mud. Believing that war implied a short sharp campaign of the type conducted by Bismarck's Prussia, people were appalled by the casualties. On the first day of the battle of the Somme the British lost about 20,000 killed and 40,000 wounded. At sea, the vast battle fleets of Britain and Germany cancelled each other out, fighting only one, indeterminate battle; but German submarines wreaked havoc among merchant ships until, at the insistence of Lloyd George (who became prime minister in December 1916), the convoy system was introduced.

Lloyd George presided over a national government, and in spite of Disraeli's dictum that the English do not love coalitions, the Conservatives continued to support him until 1923. The split in the Liberal party between pro- and anti-Lloyd George factions was thus prolonged and virtually killed the party (though it has never quite died). The Labour party had also split on the issue of pacificism, but in 1918 it was reunited on a stronger basis than before.

These changes in the political party system would no doubt have happened in some manner without the war, and in general war merely hastened processes of change that were inevitable. But it also created problems of its own. Governments in such times are inclined to make promises more extravagant than any they would contemplate in peace: the future is mortgaged to pay for the desperate present. In foreign policy, promises were made to the Italians which, not being fulfilled, contributed to the bitter disillusionment exploited so successfully by Mussolini. In the Middle East the British made contradictory promises to various Arab powers, and by simultaneously announcing support for a Jewish "national home" (the Balfour Declaration, 1917), created an insoluble problem with which they were to wrestle for nearly thirty years.

Although the British empire was actually enlarged by the results of the war, imperial rule was badly shaken. A measure of self-government and vague promises of independence to India did not satisfy the nationalist movement led by Ghandi. In 1918, 379 Indians were killed when a British commander fired on an unarmed mob at Amritsar, and the saintly Ghandi embarked on his campaign of civil disobedience. Revolution broke out in Egypt, a British protectorate, and concessions

towards self-government failed to satisfy the Egyptians; British troops remained in the country to protect the Suez Canal. At the same time the Irish crisis was reaching its climax and the seeds of future violence were sprouting in the Middle East.

The war was also costly. Expenditure had been met largely by borrowing, with the result that the pound sterling sank to about one-third of its prewar value. Capital assets were seriously depleted, and Britain was heavily in debt. But as the British Isles themselves had escaped the destruction of battle, industrial plant was largely untouched. That was a mixed blessing. Within a short time the Belgian steel industry, rebuilt from scratch on modern lines, was offering serious competition to Britain's creaking steelworks.

The government had made extra-vagant promises to its own people as well as to allies abroad, and the Bolshevik Revolution of 1917 had encouraged optimistic forecasts of a better society to discourage any inclinations of the British proletariat to follow the Russian example. After the horrors of the previous few years the British felt that good times were their due. It was—and is—widely believed that in 1914–18 the cream of a whole generation had been destroyed. People wanted to forget this disaster. But, paradoxically, they—or at any rate most of the articulate members of society—looked not towards a bright new future, but back towards a largely illusory golden past, much as people in the 17th century had looked back to an Elizabethan "golden age". The government, which in the war had assumed a blanket control of society of unprecedented extent, was eager to di-

vest itself of this ill-gotten garment. Economic restrictions were relaxed, and the way opened for euphoric speculation and rapid inflation. No centrally directed attempts were made to reconstruct industry, and a series of strikes, including a police strike, followed feeble efforts to obtain co-operation between employers and workers. The economic slump of 1921 caused high unemployment. The promises of "homes [and jobs] for heroes" made to the returning soldiers sounded increasingly hollow. Disillusionment was deepened by the feeling that corruption was rampant in high places. Though this was more a reflection of a mood than a reaction to hard facts, revelations of political scandals involving the sales of titles to socially ambitious individuals and the evidence of war profiteering and speculation provided some basis for it. There was something unhealthy too about the activities of the "Bright Young Things", frivolous young socialites commemorated in the novels of Evelyn Waugh. Far from a "home for heroes", Britain seemed more to resemble the title of T. S. Eliot's great poem (published 1922), "The Waste Land".

By the middle of the 1920s, Britain appeared a much happier place than it had in the immediate postwar period. The spirit of reconciliation, sometimes called the "Locarno spirit" after the treaties of 1925 which attempted to

settle the future affairs of Europe on the basis of arbitration, was abroad. An imperial conference in London prepared for the establishment of the "dominions" (self-governing states acknowledging the British monarch) of Australia, Canada, New Zealand and South Africa, constitutionally enacted by the Treaty of Westminster in 1931. Ghandi accepted the promise of future dominion status for India. At home, the shortlived minority Labour government of 1924 showed that the Labour party was not a gang of wild-eyed bolsheviks; Ramsay MacDonald, the Labour prime minister, even insisted on wearing ceremonial court dress. There was an improvement in the economic situation too, though it was shackled by the insistence of the Conservative government on returning the pound to the gold standard at its unrealistically high, pre-1914 value. This decision led indirectly to the General Strike of 1926.

The General Strike began as a strike in the coal-mining industry, traditionally the most troublesome source of

The young Winston Churchill campaigning for election to parliament. He switched parties twice and was generally considered untrustworthy.

industrial unrest. The announcement by the owners of a cut in wages (due to the artificially high value of the pound) was naturally resisted; the owners reacted obtusely and the government set up a committee of inquiry which contained no labour representative and no one with much experience of the coal industry. On April 26 the miners struck and the Trades Union Congress called for a partial national strike in sympathy. The government, which was well-prepared for the strike, reacted vigorously, and the result was an almost total strike of industrial workers which lasted for nine days. That the strike held as well as it did was largely thanks to Ernest Bevin and his enormous Transport and General

Workers' Union. On the other hand, the government's emergency measures worked well, and the strike failed in its basic purpose because the miners, whose strike continued or another six months, were eventually forced to surrender.

For British society, the General Strike was perhaps the most important single event of the years 1918–39. It clarified and in some respects hardened the division between Left and Right, but it also cast doubt on whether such massive campaigns of civil disobedience were a justifiable means of forcing change in a democratic society. It created much bitterness, which might have been far worse but for the policy of "masterly in-

activity" followed by Stanley Baldwin, the prime minister. It also had some comic moments. Football matches were played between police and strikers. Rival groups of students, some driving buses or trains, others picketing them, ended up drinking convivially in the same pub.

Life in the two troubled decades between the wars had its attractions, including some novel ones. Sport, especially football, became immensely popular. The cinema provided welcome relief from everyday grimness: more than 3,000 cinemas were built by 1930, many of them splendidly exotic Art-Deco palaces, now unfortunately being rapidly demolished. The British Broadcasting Corporation established

its unrivalled reputation as a kind of national aunt, entertaining, instructive, socially responsible. Motor vehicles replaced the horse, though private cars were a luxury for most people. Housing remained a perennial problem, but rapid (if often unwisely planned) building improved the lot of many. Other old problems were unsolved. Population increasingly congregated in the prosperous south-east (London topped the eight-million mark by 1930), away from the depressed areas of the north—the scene of the first industrial revolution. A large minority of the population lived in poverty. Unemployment never dropped much below one million.

The world slump of the early 1930s sent unemployment soaring, reaching a peak of nearly four million. The Labour government, which had the misfortune to come to power shortly before the Wall Street crash of October 1929, was like other governments bewildered by the crisis. A maverick politician named Oswald Mosley put forward a promising plan, but it was rejected and he went off in disgust to found a new, fascist party. What little the government did was along the right lines, as recommended by the economist John Maynard Keynes, but its efforts were few and feeble, its confidence frail. A political crisis in 1931

resulted in the formation of a national government, with Ramsay MacDonald continuing as premier though repudiated by most of the parliamentary Labour party. At a general election, the national government secured overwhelming popular approval.

The real victor of the crisis of 1931 was the Conservative leader, Stanley Baldwin, who succeeded MacDonald as prime minister in 1935. He and MacDonald conducted the government of the country, in the words of David Thomson, "like a sedate and leisurely firm of comfortable family solicitors". The rose-growing, pipe-smoking, phlegmatic Baldwin has received an unduly bad press form historians, though the charge that he deliberately rejected rearmament for the sake of party advantage has been largely demolished: in any case, Britain's tardiness in rearming was ultimately an advantage, since earlier re-equipment would likely have resulted in obsolete weaponry in September 1939. Baldwin, who preferred (or said he preferred) the leisurely life of the countryside, mirrored a popular preoccupation—the desire to "get away from it all", to go off somewhere with knapsack or bicycle, far away from the ribbon development of the suburbs and the new "functional" buildings of

the towns, far from the grim evidence of unemployment and stagnation.

By 1933, the economy was showing signs of recovery as a result, not of the policy of the national government which rejected Keynes's advice to spend lavishly, but of world trends, especially the fall in commodity prices. But relief came chiefly to the areas least in need: in the depressed north–east and north-west unemployment remained high and living standards, in spite of unemployment pay, dreadfully low. The more comfortable members of society were shaken by outbreaks of political violence by extreme groups on the Left and Right. Mosley's black-shirted fascists made more noise than their numbers warranted, but clashes were so frequent that extra powers were given to the police to deal with political demonstrations.

Amid this turbulence, the monarchy at least seemed a centre of stability. George V (1910–36) was old-fashioned in outlook and limited in intelligence, but he was solid, sensible, quintessentially honest and, to his own surprise, popular. After his death, however, even the island of security represented by the monarchy appeared to be sinking when the handsome young Edward VIII informed his advisers that he would be unable to perform his kingly duties without the regal support of a twice-married American woman, Mrs Simpson. The scandal, long concealed, caused a tremendous sensation, with the public taking sides for and against the King. Baldwin manoeuvred him into abdication, making way for his far more suitable younger brother, George VI (1936–52).

Britain's concern with its own affairs in the 1930s helps to account for the feebleness of British foreign policy. Britain paid lip-service to the League of Nations and "collective security" but scouted its own principles in the disreputable Hoare-Laval Pact, which acknowledged Italian suzerainty in most of Ethiopia. The mood of the country was pacifist: Winston Churchill, thundering dire warnings of what Germany was up to, was regarded as a dangerous hawk. People did not want to know: they were frightened by the idea of war, but they did not know how it was to be prevented. There were signs of growing resolution in 1935 when Ernest Bevin's brutal speech at the Labour party conference ousted the pacifist George Lansbury from leadership of the party, but the predominant national mood was intensely anti-war, and remained so up to September 1939. The Rome-Berlin axis stimulated no serious counter-move in Britain; the Spanish civil war was officially disregarded. The replacement of Baldwin by Neville Chamberlain (1937), who had the reputation of a political strong man, made no difference to policy. Like many of his generation, Chamberlain was obsessed by the horror of the First World War and determined to avoid its repetition at almost any cost. The *Anschluss* was greeted by mild protests only, and there was never much question of saving the Czechs—"a far-

away . . . people", in Chamberlain's description, "of whom we know nothing".

What ended the policy of appeasement was the German march into Prague in March 1939, in blatant disregard of the Munich agreement for which Chamberlain had struggled so hard six months before. In a flurried reversal of policy, Britain issued guarantees right and left to all countries threatened by Hitler's aggression. Ef-

forts were made to secure a Soviet alliance, until Stalin shocked the West, including Western Communists, by signing a non-aggression pact with Hitler. The German invasion of Poland a week later invited a declaration of war by Britain and France.

Chamberlain hung on to the premiership until May 1940, when he was replaced by Winston Churchill—a striking case of the hour producing the man, for Churchill's move to No 10

Downing Street coincided with the end of the "phoney war" and the beginning of a period of rapid German conquest. The British Expeditionary Force was driven out of Europe and escaped by the skin of its teeth from the beaches of Dunkirk; every little yacht and pleasure cruiser available made the Channel crossing to take off British and French troops. Churchill, telling the people he had nothing to offer but "blood, toil, tears and sweat", typefied a new mood–the "spirit of Dunkirk". No victory ever did so much for national morale as that defeat. The hysteria of the thirties, born of fear and bewilderment, was banished, and was replaced by gritty, realistic determination.

After the fall of France, Hitler turned towards the last significant opponent remaining. The Battle of Britain was perhaps the decisive turning point of the war, for the attack of the *Luftwaffe*, first on ports and shippings, then on airfields, finally on London, was repulsed, and the threat of invasion averted; thus Hitler failed to establish German hegemony in Western Europe before the inevitable conflict with greater foes.

Although the British like to think of the Battle of Britain as the gallant victory of "the Few" (fighter pilots) against the vast ranks of the *Luftwaffe,* the overall odds were in fact fairly even. The British were outnumbered in terms of aeroplanes and pilots, but the Spitfire was a vastly superior aircraft to anything the Germans could put in British skies, and Britain had the enormous advantage of radar, which gave early warning of the size and direction of German attacks. All the same, if the attack on airfields had been continued for a short time longer, the Royal Air Force might have been grounded. As it was, a German invasion became impossible after September 1940, though heavy bombing attacks on London and other industrial cities, notably Coventry, continued.

The repulse of the *Luftwaffe* did nothing to check the inexorable German advance in Europe, and 1941 was a disastrous year as the German armies rolled through south-east Europe. But the German attack on Russia and the Japanese assault on Pearl Harbor brought the vast resources of the Soviet Union and the United States into the fight against Hitler and made the ultimate defeat of Germany certain.

The British co-operated closely and, on the whole, remarkably amiably with the Americans. The greatest feat of British arms was Montgomery's victory over Rommel's Afrika Korps et El Alamein in 1942. A year later the RAF was mounting huge bombing attacks on German industry—and cities. The most frightful of these air raids destroyed the lovely city of Dresden in 1945, with colossal civilian casualties.

Meanwhile, Italy had been forced out of the war and, in June 1944, the long-demanded Second Front was opened with the allied landings in Normandy. The attack met tremendous German resistance, while London suffered from frightening new weapons, the V-1 and V-2 rockets. In February 1945 the allied leaders met at Yalta, where Stalin was unnecessarily bribed with promises of territory. In April the first United Nations meeting assembled in San Francisco, and in May the war in Europe ended. In the Far East the Japanese had been compelled to retreat from their conquests in Burma and South-East Asia, and the atomic bomb forced their surrender in August.

12 Readjustment 1945-1975

The British people's retrospective view of the Second World War makes an interesting contrast with their view of the First. Although civilian casualties were higher in the second war, total casualties were much lower, and while the First World War had turned out to be in every way a vastly worse experience than people had expected when it began, the Second was—for the British—less dreadful than they had been warned to expect. Moreover, the British felt justifiably proud of themselves. Although they played a subsidiary role in the later stages, in the most dangerous period of the war they had, with Commonwealth aid, stood alone against Nazi aggression. Churchill, the BBC and the spirit of Dunkerque had given the nation a powerful sense of unity which people old enough still remember with nostalgic affection (though they exaggerate the national unity: more man-hours were lost through strikes in 1943–44 than in some years of peace).

In material terms, Britain emerged from the Second World War a heavy loser. So vast were British debts, especially in dollars, that in economic terms Britain was hardly more than the "49th State" that people critical of the enormous American influence on cultural life called it. The only bright spot in the economic picture was the agricultural boom resulting from wartime demand, which made Britain again a leader in farming methods and productivity.

The second war, like the first, encouraged social developments already in progress and speeded up the rate of change. After 1918 people felt they had been cheated of the just society they had expected; they were more wary and determined in 1945. The election of a Labour government in the last months of the war, though a slap in the face for Churchill, demonstrated the national awareness that new times had arrived and new measures were needed. There was no nostalgia for pre-war days. The thirties aroused only bitter memories of the slump.

The basis for the Welfare State introduced by the Labour government between 1945 and 1950 had been laid by the Beveridge Report (named after the chairman of the parliamentary committee that produced it) as early as 1942. The progressive Education Act of 1944 had been fathered by a Conservative, R. A. Butler, and the payment of family allowances at a fixed rate per child had also been introduced while Churchill was still in power. Thus the mandate of the Labour government was plain.

Labour had a substantial majority in parliament and, for the first time, highly experienced leaders in the cabinet, notably Clement Attlee, prime minister, and Ernest Bevin, foreign minister. The first major legislation was concerned with the nationalisation of the power and transport industries. This provoked little opposition. Many of the industries concerned were already run as public or semi-public corporations, and all except a few die-hards admitted that nationalisation of the coal industry, in particular, was long overdue. Steel was more controversial, and when the Conservatives came to power in 1951 they partially, and temporarily, returned it to private ownership. On the whole, nationalization had little effect on anyone involved, though in the long term it came to be held responsible for over-manning and poor management.

The extension of social security had a far greater effect on society. Notable advances were made in national insurance, publicly owned housing and

education, but without doubt the greatest single achievement in the whole area of social welfare was the creation of a national health service (1948). The child of the fiery Welsh radical, Aneurin Bevan, it provided all necessary medical treatment free. Later, small charges were introduced for eye-glasses, false teeth and some medicines, provoking the resignation of Bevan and his supporters, including Harold Wilson. Since then, medical treatment has become still less "free"; in the 1970s the whole service appeared to be not far short of a serious breakdown, with doctors operating a go-slow and most other professional groups voicing discontent of one kind or another. Part of the trouble stemmed from Bevan's concession to the doctors which permitted them to treat private (i.e. fee-paying) patients in state hospitals. The attempt to run a socialist state system alongside a private or semi-private one, was to cause trouble for future Labour governments in areas besides health, notably education.

Apart from the legislative achievements of the Labour government in the late 1940s, life in Britain was rather grey. "Austerity" was the watchword, and the sternly puritanical countenance of the Chancellor of the Exchequer, Stafford Cripps, seemed to fit the times. The huge dollar debt, rising inflation and an unhealthy balance of payments presented severe problems, only partly alleviated by aid through the American Marshall Plan (1947). The accustomed scarcities of wartime were not easily overcome: bread was rationed in 1947 though it had never been rationed during the war. However, the government was thoroughly successful in what has always been a major preoccupation of the Labour party since the 1930s: the maintenance of full employment.

The measures of austerity which were forced upon the government did not make it popular, and in spite of its excellent legislative record, its majority was seriously reduced in the election of 1950. Other difficulties—war in Korea, ill-health or resignation of leading ministers—made the government's task so difficult that a new election was called in 1951. This time the Conservatives gained a narrow majority although, thanks to the peculiarities of the electoral system, the Labour party had more votes. Churchill returned to No 10 Downing Street at the age of 77. Suffering a stroke soon afterwards, he was no longer capable of the job, but who could tell the saviour of his country that he was past it? His patient heir apparent, Anthony Eden, had to wait until early 1955 for Churchill's retirement.

There was no question of the Conservatives repealing Labour's welfare legislation. Indeed, with growing prosperity in the 1950s, the ideological differences between the two parties seemed slight, giving rise to the expression "Butskellism" (a combination of the names of R. A. Butler, leader of the Conservatives' liberal wing, and Hugh Gaitskell, Attlee's successor as Labour leader). The Labour party in Britain, although it is essentially the party of the trade unions and has always possessed a vociferous Left-wing, socialist element, is also the descendant of the old Liberal party of Gladstone and Lloyd George. In another country, it would be called a 'social-democratic' party. Similarly the liberal element among the Conservatives, usually dominant, has preserved the party of Peel and Disraeli as a popular party able to attract many working-class votes.

The accession of Elizabeth II was greeted with great excitement in 1952, but the second "golden age" has not yet materialised.

The Second World War everywhere advanced the growing spirit of nationalism and egalitarianism. It was clear that, even without the anti-imperialism of the United States and the Soviet Union, the British empire would by some means be dismantled. That India, a country containing nearly 20 per cent of the world's population, should be independent was fairly widely agreed (Churchill was the most notable dissenter), and the real question was how could independence be managed? In particular, how were the violently antagonistic Hindus and Muslims to be reconciled? Attlee made the shrewd choice of Lord Mountbatten, a grandson of Queen Victoria, to carry out the difficult task of divorcing Britain from the Raj. Largely by the force of his character, Mountbatten secured agreement to a partition of the country. It was not accomplished without violence and bloodshed, and subsequent events have shown that the creation of Pakistan in two distinct parts was an unworkable arrangement, but it is generally agreed that any other course of action would have had more dreadful results. India and Pakistan became dominions within the Commonwealth in 1947; the subsequent decision to become republics made constitutional alterations in the Commonwealth necessary, converting it into an association of totally independent states with the British monarch as head of the Commonwealth but not (or not necessarily) head of any individual state.

Ceylon (Sri Lanka) and Burma also became independent in 1947; no objection was raised when Burma rejected Commonwealth membership. In Malaya, the authorities had to deal with a Communist guerilla campaign. Though not to be compared with the situation of the United States in South Vietnam, the British had some reason for self-congratulation when the Malaya "emergency" ended in success for the forces of democracy. The Federation of Malaysia gained independence in 1957.

The announcement that Britain intended to withdraw from Palestine, which it administered under a mandate from the old League of Nations, was widely disbelieved in spite of the evidence which India provided that Britain's policy of imperial disengagement was sincere. The last months of British rule in Palestine were sordid, with some cases of fascist behaviour by troops embittered by acts of terrorism against them. British withdrawal (ahead of schedule) was followed by Arab attack, Zionist victory, and the foundation of the modern state of Israel within borders wider than the United Nations partition plan had provided.

Among Britain's African possessions, the Gold Coast led the way. It was politically a more coherent entity than other African colonies, it was economically prosperous, and it had a dynamic leader in Kwame Nkrumah, who became prime minister in 1951. As Ghana, the country achieved full

Below: Grim comment from Jeremiah in Belfast: "The harvest is past, the summer is ended, and we are not saved".

independence in 1957, followed within a few years by other African states. Disengagement was seldom achieved with perfect smoothness. The Mau Mau campaign in Kenya cost hundreds of lives between 1952 and 1956, and most of the men who were to become respected statesmen and leaders of the Commonwealth served time in British prisons. In Rhodesia independence was delayed because the substantial white population was unwilling to concede political equality to black Rhodesians. Finally, the whites made a unilateral declaration of independence (1965) which, having forsworn military measures, Britain was unable to contest.

Another notorious trouble-spot was Cyprus, where Greek Cypriots favouring *enosis* (union with Greece) conducted a guerilla campaign against the British. A compromise was reached which lasted just long enough for the foundation of the independent state of Cyprus in 1960.

In spite of these individual problems, frequently not of its own making, Britain succeeded in shedding its imperial connections with surprisingly

little conflict or bitterness. Many things might have been better managed, but none of the death throes of the British empire compared with the agonies of the French experience in Algeria, the Belgian legacy in the Congo (Zaire), or Portugal's in Angola. Most ex-colonies chose to remain within the remodelled Commonwealth of Nations, from which the name "British" was dropped and, although the Commonwealth had little—and

has come to have less–practical significance, it was at least a symbol of interracial fellowship, besides offering some comfort to those in Britain who regretted the disappearance of closer connections.

Although Britain showed an enlightened attitude to imperial disengagement, the odd atavistic convulsion occurred, most memorably in 1956.

With rapidly growing prosperity at home and a solid victory in the election of 1955, the Eden government confronted its most intractable problems abroad—in Kenya, in Cyprus (where some nasty cases of British repression were exposed), and the Middle East, where Communist influence was moving into the vacuum left by Western withdrawal. Eden seemed to be just the man to deal with these problems, for he was the most experienced foreign minister of the century: he had held that office before the Second World War and enjoyed the distinction of having resigned in protest against Chamberlain's policy. But it is possible to learn the lessons of the past too well. When Nasser nationalised

Left: British troops lining up civilians during security operations in Ulster.
Below: Republican sympathisers in Northern Ireland set up temporary "no-go" areas in Roman Catholic districts of Belfast and Londonderry which British troops and police did not enter.

the Suez Canal in 1956 in defiance of international agreements, Eden saw him as a new Hitler embarking on a policy of raw aggression. The Suez Canal had certainly been a vital link in Britain's imperial communications, but to speak of Nasser placing a "thumb on our windpipe" in 1956 was to exaggerate Britain's vulnerability. However, when international efforts to reach agreement failed, Britain and France secretly decided on military occupation of the Canal, timing their invasion to coincide with an Israeli attack on Egypt.

Eden's extraordinary reversion to Palmerstonian tactics aroused intense opposition. In the United Nations the Soviet Union and the United States both condemned the Anglo-French occupation. At home it was greeted with outrage by almost the whole Labour party and, less vociferously, by many Conservatives; two junior ministers resigned. Even if the British and the French had been prepared to face the near-universal hostility of the rest of the world, the rapid fall in Britain's gold reserves would have compelled swift withdrawal. A UN peace-keep-

ing force took over, but the encouragement that this might give to those who put their faith in the UN as a force for international justice was blighted by the simultaneous suppression of Hungary by the Soviet Union.

Suez finished Eden's career (his health had been fragile for some years), but did little damage to the Conservative party. Harold Macmillan, the most capable peace-time prime minister since Baldwin, defeated Butler in a contest for the party leadership, and commenced his misleadingly bland direction of the nation's affairs in what became known as the "age of affluence".

Britain again benefitted in the 1950s from world developments, especially the fall in commodity prices, to which the British economy is always particularly sensitive. Greater prosperity was especially obvious among those whom Lord Salisbury had once called "the middling sort of people", skilled and "white-collar" workers who usually owned a car and a house where their fathers had ridden a bicycle and rented. In spite of persistent pockets of poverty and endemic industrial

unrest, manifest in large strikes, the great majority were richer than ever before, and living standards were still rising. "You've never had it so good" was the unattractive slogan of the Conservatives under Macmillan.

But conspicuous consumer spending was not matched by investment and the institutions of the welfare state deteriorated through declining government support. The national health service suffered from a growing shortage of doctors, nurses and hospitals, though Enoch Powell's spell as minister of health in 1962–64 made some improvement. Old-age pensions lagged behind wages. Persistent difficulties in controlling inflation and maintaining a healthy balance of trade pointed to a fundamental weakness in the economy, and the government's resort to "stop-go" economic tactics—expansion one year, contraction the next—not only irritated the public but revealed the absence of basic long-term policy. By 1962 the image of "Supermac" was looking tarnished: a sensational scandal involving sex and spies, and some ruthless chopping and changing of cabinet ministers left a bad

dustrial disturbance. But that is no more than a theory. The effects may have been slighter than might be reasonably supposed. The mass of the population never gave much thought to the empire anyway, and remains contentedly ignorant about the rest of the world. One of the saddest developments of the 1960s was the enactment of laws restricting, and in the end virtually banning, the immigration of Commonwealth citizens. In view of the numbers entering the country—mainly West Indians in the early 1950s, later more from India and Pakistan—such legislation was inevitable, but it was highly destructive of idealistic views of the Commonwealth.

Britain's long-standing economic handicaps did not vanish in the "age of affluence", but they were more easily ignored. In the 1960s, a mood of gay frivolity appeared to have possessed the country. The boutiques of Carnaby Street and the King's Road and the pop records of the Beatles made England the centre of youthful fashion and entertainment. Though vastly exaggerated by the communications media, this development was pleasant as well as unexpected, even if it did seem at times, as Jonathan Miller remarked, that the British Isles were about to sink giggling into the sea. Others were more sternly disapproving, and adumbrated an ethical problem. They drew attention to continuing areas of deprivation; to a widening gap, even under the Labour government, between the very poor and the rest of the community; to a disregard for the problems of the Third World; to rising crime, especially violent crime among young people. The Church appeared to be barely floating in a sea of indifference, while political leaders offered no goal except

taste. Having taken a major part in the negotiation of the nuclear test-ban treaty (1963), which he regarded as the high point of his career, Macmillan resigned. His successor, Sir Alec Douglas-Home, failed to arrest the popular swing towards the Labour party under Harold Wilson, who narrowly won power in 1964 and, by calling a new election the following year, substantially increased his majority.

The period after the Second World War was one of change and upheaval in cultural life. The old class structure, which had acquired rigidity in Victorian times largely through the middle-class education provided by the "public" (in fact they are "private") schools, was clearly disintegrating as society became more fairly organized, with smaller differ-

entials in income, better state education and more democratic institutions. The new affluence of the 1950s and 1960s fostered the teenager as a numerous and commercially important consumer. The general advance of allegedly American values and social habits affected everything from eating to sex; old taboos fell rapidly. Some of the best work of the Wilson government of 1964–70 was its legislation on homosexuality, censorship, and other matters leading to a more tolerant society.

The psychological effects of Britain's swift divestment of the trappings of colonialism are hard to judge. Foreigners sometimes diagnosed a traumatic experience in the loss of empire which accounted for the persistent problems of low investment and in-

a higher standard of living, and in the 1970s even that had to be abandoned.

In their relations with the rest of the world after 1945, the British were slow to realise how much power and influence they had lost. An independent foreign policy was no longer possible and, as the United Nations failed to fulfil idealistic hopes for world order, Britain had to decide where its loyalty, or its best interests, lay: with the Commonwealth, with the United States, or with democratic Europe. These three alternatives were not mutually exclusive. The Americans were eager to see Britain as a leader of a united Western Europe, and for reasons of defence alone, Britain (and Western Europe) was dependent on the United States alliance. But Labour distrusted moves towards European unity which drew much of their support from capitalist and Roman Catholic parties on the continent, while Conservatives and Socialists alike emphasised Commonwealth allegiances and expressed fears for British sovereignty.

Thus the Treaty of Rome (1957) aroused little enthusiasm: only the tiny Liberal party advocated British membership of the European Economic Community. Instead, Britain formed a much looser economic association (the European Free Trade Association) with six countries outside the EEC. But subsequently opinion began to turn in favour of the EEC as a result of the startling economic progress of its members, and in 1961 Edward Heath was appointed to negotiate British membership. His efforts were brought to an abrupt close by De Gaulle's uncompromising rejection of British membership in 1963, but when the French president resigned six years later, discussions were resumed. Basic agreement was reached in 1971 and on

1 January 1973 Heath, who had become prime minister in 1970, triumphantly led the country "into Europe". Meanwhile, Labour leaders, influenced by trade-union hostility to the EEC, had become doubtful. Wilson demanded renegotiation of the terms of entry and a nationwide referendum on the results. This was carried out after Labour returned to power in 1974. The argument generated a great deal of publicity but the final result—overwhelming public approval—was hardly in doubt. Thus Britain, after much hesitation, finally threw in its lot with Europe. It became again what it had been in the 15th century—a small, not very prosperous country on the edge of Europe.

The fuss over EEC membership had obscured more urgent problems. In spite of solid achievements in social affairs, especially education, the Labour government of 1964–70 failed to overcome Britain's economic difficulties. An increasingly troublesome symptom was loss of production through strikes, especially unofficial strikes. Labour legislation to regulate industrial relations was blocked by trade-union pressure, but in 1971 Heath's government set up a special industrial court to make contracts between employers and workers enforceable at law. The Conservative act aroused furious opposition and merely aggravated the fundamental problems. Strikes increased, and when the coal miners challenged a government wage "freeze", Heath called a general election to determine "who rules Britain" (i.e. the trade unions or the gov-

Below: Heath signs Britain into the EEC. Flanking him are Sir Alec Douglas Home, foreign secretary, and Geoffrey Rippon (at right), who negotiated the agreement.

After centuries of more or less deliberate isolation, Britain lines up with its European neighbours.

ernment?). The gamble did not work, Labour returned to power, and the Conservative Industrial Relations Act was swiftly removed from the statute book. But by 1975, steadily rising unemployment together with an annual rate of inflation exceeding 25 per cent enforced more reasonable attitudes in industrial relations. Wilson's government succeeded in gaining Trades Union Congress co-operation to restrict wage increases, and with firms in serious trouble all over the country, strikes became fewer.

A horrible wound was reopened in these years by the increase of terrorist activity in Northern Ireland. The IRA (Irish Republican Army), a terrorist organization banned in Eire as well as Northern Ireland, became increasingly active in Belfast, Londonderry and border areas. Ostensibly operating in

defence of the Roman Catholic minority in Northern Ireland, it provoked similar crimes of murder and intimidation by extremist Protestant groups. In 1969 British troops were sent in to keep the peace, but they failed to obtain sufficient co-operation from the civilian population to stop the violence which, in the shape of random bombings and assassinations, spread to England also.

Ironically, while the Protestant majority in Northern Ireland clung to their right to remain a part of the United Kingdom, separatism was growing stronger in Scotland and Wales. Frightened by the electoral successes of the Scottish National party, the government made proposals to give both countries greater autonomy in local affairs, though the proposals were widely criticised and failed

in their tacit purpose to deflate the nationalist balloon in the "Celtic fringe".

By the middle of the 1970s it was painfully obvious that not only was the age of affluence over (living standards declined in 1975 for the first time since the Second World War), but that Britain's economy was in a state of genuine crisis. Although the recession, which combined inflation and stagnation in a noxious blend that economists could not satisfactorily explain, was worldwide, Britains suffered more severely than its neighbours. The rate of inflation was more than double that of France, Germany or the Benelux countries, and the cost of imports regularly exceeded the value of exports. Blame for this situation was variously ascribed to Britain's vulnerability to rising commodity prices; to wage rises exceeding the rise in the cost of living; to the old problems of low industrial investment and outdated methods of production; to excessive government spending on social services. More controversially, industrial management in both the private and public sectors of the economy was frequently criticised as incompetent, and the civil service, of which the British had long been rightly proud, was said to be over-staffed, complacent and, on occasions, irresponsible.

In spite of the somewhat grim situation of Britain in the 1970s, some causes for hope in the future could be discerned. In the long term, Britain was well-provided with fossil fuels: besides its large coal reserves, the exploitation of submarine deposits of oil and gas was expected to make the country a net exporter of fuels in the 1980s. Indeed, the first dribble of North Sea oil was seen, perhaps too optimistically, as the light on the horizon that promises a glorious dawn.

Britain also possessed large reserves of skilled manpower. If a solution to the problem of industrial unrest could be found, if management could be improved and industrial processes streamlined, there was no reason why the British should not improve their position among leading manufacturing nations. London was still a ma-jor financial capital, and the poor export performance of manufacturing was not parallelled by the important "invisible" exports of insurance and investment banking.

However Britain, like other countries, is no longer master of its own destinies—if it ever was. The future really depends on factors far out-side British control, perhaps out of anyone's control. But insofar as the future is deliberately fashioned by man, the British will without doubt make a contribution; for it is unlikely that Britain's relegation to a modest position in the tables of political and economic power will put an end to the creativity and energy of the British.

Chronology

1947	Independence of India: other colonies follow
1953	Mount Everest climbed by Commonwealth expedition
1956	Invasion of Suez; British forced to withdraw after universal condemnation
1962	First record of the Beatles, Liverpool pop music group
1965	Rhodesia makes unilateral declaration of independence
1969	British troops sent to Northern Ireland
1970	Discovery of oil in the North Sea
1973	Britain joins the European Economic Community
1977	Queen Elizabeth II celebrates silver jubilee of her reign